A Handbook for Conscious Living
in Chaotic Times

it's time

A Handbook for Conscious Living in Chaotic Times

Gail Lynn

Synthia Andrews, N.D. · Penny Kelly · Suzy Miller, M.Ed.
Steven A. Ross, Ph.D. · Mona Sobhani, Ph.D. · Ani Williams
Deborah Cambio · Sarah Cotterill · Charles Monroe, Jr.

Edited by Sandie Sedgbeer

Copyright © 2025 by Gail Lynn

All rights reserved. No part of this book may be reproduced by any mechanical, photographic, or electronic process, or in the form of a phonographic recording; nor may it be stored in a retrieval system, transmitted, or otherwise be copied for public or private use—other than for "fair use" as brief quotations embodied in articles and reviews—without prior written permission of the publisher.

Disclaimer

The statements made by the author and any recommendations of services in this book are not intended to diagnose, treat, cure or prevent any disease. Testimonials regarding the technology are voluntarily given and do not represent the opinions of the author. The information provided and knowledge and experiences shared by the author are not intended to be a substitute for professional medical advice, diagnosis, or treatment.

ISBN 978-1-7343783-4-4 (print)
ISBN 978-1-7343783-6-8 (ebook)

10 9 8 7 6 5 4 3 2 1

Edited by Sandie Sedgbeer
Cover design and interior layout by Damian Keenan
This book was typeset in Adobe Garamond Pro, Museo and Calluna Sans with ITC Century Std Book Condensed and Barlow Condensed used as display typefaces

You can get in touch with the author of this book using the contact form on her website at **www.harmonicegg.com**

Contents

Editor's Note *by Sandie Sedgbeer* 9

Prologue *by Gail Lynn* 11

Introduction: Dispelling the Illusion of Powerlessness
by Gail Lynn 13

1 **Introducing Penny Kelly** 17
   A New Beginning *by Penny Kelly* 19
   Gail's Conscious Living Challenge 33

2 **Introducing Synthia Andrews, N.D.** 36
   Subtle Energy Work: The Language of the Heart
   by Synthia Andrews, N.D. 37
   Gail's Conscious Living Challenge 52

3 **Introducing Steven A. Ross Ph.D.** 55
   Timeless Wisdom for a Modern World
   by Steven A. Ross, Ph.D. 57
   Who is Colorblind? Excerpted from "And Nothing Happened –
   But You Can Make it Happen" *by Steven A. Ross, Ph.D.* 68
   Gail's Conscious Living Challenge 80

4 **Introducing Ani Williams** 83
   Rewriting Our Story, Recreating Our World
   An interview with Ani Williams *by Sandie Sedgbeer* 84
   Gail's Conscious Living Challenge 98

5 **Introducing Sarah Cotterill** 100
   Moving From the Love of Power to the Power of Love
   by Sarah Cotterill 101
   Gail's Conscious Living Challenge 111

6 **Introducing Mona Sobhani, Ph.D.** 114
    When Two Worlds Collide: A Neuroscientist's Accidental
       Spiritual Awakening *by Mona Sobhani, Ph.D.* 115
    Gail's Conscious Living Challenge 124

7 **Introducing Charles Monroe, Jr.** 127
    Your Body Knows How to Heal Itself *by Charles Monroe, Jr.* 128
    Gail's Conscious Living Challenge 139

8 **Introducing Deborah Cambio** 141
    Beyond Pills and Procedures: What Modern Medicine Misses
       by Deborah Cambio 143
    Gail's Conscious Living Challenge 149

9 **Introducing Suzy Miller** 151
    Lessons in Love *by Suzy Miller, M.Ed.* 152
    Gail's Conscious Living Challenge: 161

    EPILOGUE: It's Time 163

APPENDICES

I 10 Steps to Reinventing Our World
    by Penny Kelly 171

II A Meditation for Mother Earth – Renewing Your Connection
    to Mother Earth – *A Meditation with Penny Kelly* 173

III Techniques for Bio-hacking Anxiety
    by Dr. Synthia Andrews 176

IV A Daily Guide for Living in Love
    by Steven A. Ross, Ph.D. 180

V	Breathing and Toning for Well-being	
	by Ani Williams	184
VI	The Heart Reconnection Journey: Reclaiming Your Power	188
	A Simple Daily Practice to Transform Your Story	
	by Sarah Cotterill	188
VII	Bilateral Stimulation: A Simple Way to Process Your Emotions	
	by Mona Sobhani, Ph.D.	191
VIII	Simple Techniques to Cultivate Love, Forgiveness & Gratitude	
	by Charles Monroe, Jr.	193
IX	The Triangle: A Conscious Communication Tool	
	by Deborah Cambio	194
X	What is Mirroring? How Does it Work? And Why Should You Care?	
	by Suzy Miller	197
	About the Author	200

Editor's Note

While filming *It's Time*, we had the incredible opportunity to sit down with each of the experts featured in this book and capture hours of meaningful, eye-opening conversations. Sadly, there just wasn't enough time to include all their knowledge, wisdom, and experience.

The good news? Our contributors have generously shared some bonus material to accompany their chapters—additional insights, helpful tools and techniques, meditations, and personal reflections. Some of it expands on what they shared in the movie and wrote about here, and some offers fresh ways to apply their ideas in your everyday life.

We're truly honored to share this added wisdom with you as a series of Appendices to complement the book and the film. We hope these offerings spark inspiration, deepen your understanding, and support you on your journey of transformation.

Prologue

There are moments in history when everything changes—when humanity stands at a crossroads so profound that what comes next is no longer a question of chance, but a question of choice.

This is one of those moments when the choices we make will determine whether we evolve or disappear.

It has happened before. Civilizations have risen, grown powerful, and then collapsed under the weight of their own corruption, greed, and refusal to adapt. The Roman Empire. The Mayans. Ancient Egypt. The fall of these once-great societies wasn't random. It was the result of **choices**—the choice to ignore the warning signs, the choice to turn away from truth, the choice to remain comfortable inside a dying system rather than forging a new path.

And now, here we are.

We are standing at the edge of an era that will define the future of our species and our planet. The world as we knew it is crumbling before our eyes. The institutions we were taught to trust—our governments, our healthcare, our education systems, our economies—have been revealed as hollow structures, built on deception, control, and profit over people. The food supply is poisoned. The media is weaponized. The systems that were supposed to protect us have enslaved us instead.

Yet the greatest illusion—the lie so deeply ingrained that most of us never question it—is that *you* are powerless to change any of this. That you are just one small person in an overwhelming world, and that your voice, your choices, your thoughts, and your actions don't matter.

That is the biggest deception of all.

You are not powerless. You are not insignificant. You are not here to be controlled, manipulated, or kept small—a passive observer in a collapsing world. You are here to **wake up, break free, and reclaim your innate power** as a creator of reality.

This book will not sugarcoat reality. It will not coddle you with empty reassurances. It will not tell you that everything will be okay if you just think happy thoughts. It is here to challenge you, shake you, push you to remember who you are.

Because the future is not written in stone—it is being written **by us, right now.**

This is our moment of choice: **evolution or extinction.**

Do we continue down the road of passive conformity, allowing fear, division, and destruction to dictate our fate? Or do we rise together, break the chains of illusion, and step fully into the truth of who we are—divine beings having a human experience—and use our power to rewrite the story of humanity?

This is our defining moment. **The only question that remains is: What will you choose?**

Introduction

Dispelling the Illusion of Powerlessness

by Gail Lynn

For generations, we have been sold a story—one so deeply ingrained that it operates beneath our conscious awareness. It tells us that we are **small, separate, and powerless.** That the world is too big, the problems too vast, and the systems too entrenched and unshakable for **one person to make a difference.**

This story is a lie. A carefully constructed illusion designed to keep us compliant, to keep us dependent on the very systems that exploit us—the **governments, corporations, and institutions** that continually fail to provide the solutions humanity needs. They have poisoned our bodies, dulled our minds, and chained our spirits in fear.

Think about it:

- **The healthcare industry** thrives because we believe we must hand over our health to an external authority, rather than learning to heal ourselves.

- **Governments** convince us that they exist to "serve the people," yet they manufacture division, feed us fear, and strip away our sovereignty and freedoms under the guise of protection.

- **The food industry** profits from poisoning our bodies with chemicals and synthetic substances, while we buy what they sell, blindly consuming what is marketed as "normal."

- **The media** shapes our thoughts, tells us what to believe, who to hate, and what to fear—ensuring we never question who is really pulling the strings.

Every aspect of our reality has been engineered to control us. And the only reason this system works is *because we allow it to.*

But here's the truth: *We* **are the system.**

The moment we recognize this—truly recognize it—is the moment everything changes. Because the only way these systems thrive is through *our compliance*.

This is not about politics. It's not about left or right, conspiracy or mainstream. It's about opening our eyes and minds to the invisible chains that have kept humanity in a cycle of suffering for centuries and making the conscious decision to step out of that illusion.

The Breaking Point

We are at a breaking point. A reckoning.

Look around. The cracks in the system are no longer subtle—they are gaping holes. People are waking up. The narratives are unraveling. The illusion is beginning to crumble.

Yet so many still cling to it. **Why?**

Because **awakening is hard.** It means facing the truth that we have been deceived. It means taking responsibility for our role in maintaining the system. It means **owning our power,** and for many, that is terrifying.

But here's the reality:

- **No one is coming to save you.** The government won't. The corporations won't. The institutions won't.

- **You are not a victim.** Life is not *happening to* you—it is *responding to* you. Your choices, your thoughts, your actions create your reality.

- **Healing is your responsibility.** Trauma is real. Loss is painful. But remaining stuck in the past serves no one. The world doesn't need more wounded people waiting to be saved. It needs warriors willing to rise.

So, Where do You Start?

Own Your Power—Stop waiting for someone to "fix" the world. **You are the one you've been waiting for.**

Recognize the Illusion of Separation—We have been taught to fear and judge each other. But we are not separate. We are one human tribe.

Break the Trauma Cycle—Most people are emotionally stuck in the past, reliving old wounds instead of healing and evolving. I repeat, no one is coming to save you. It's time to do the work.

A New Story for Humanity

This is not a time for passive hope. It is a time for active awakening. If we want to change the world, we must start with *ourselves*.

To evolve as a species, we must stop clinging to outdated beliefs, societal programming, and the wounds of the past. We must let go of the illusion of separation. The idea that we are alone, divided, powerless.

We are none of those things. We are creators. We are powerful beyond measure. We are here now, because we chose to be.

It's time to step fully into our conscious, creative power and take responsibility for the world we are co-creating.

And that means we have work to do.

This book is not just about understanding what is wrong with the world—it is a call to those who feel the pull of something greater. Who know, deep inside that they came here for a reason. It is about remembering what is possible. About reclaiming our birthright as conscious, energetic beings, stepping into truth, and using that power to shape a new reality and co-create the greatest transformation in human history.

Each chapter offers an in-depth exploration of the crucial insights, evidence, and practical wisdom shared by the leading experts featured in my documentary film, *It's Time*.... These thought leaders, who come from diverse fields such as cognitive neuroscience, medical law, agriculture, nutrition, metaphysics, and energy healing, shared powerful truths that we couldn't fully include within the film's time constraints. In this text, their knowledge is preserved and expanded upon, providing you with practical tools and a deeper understanding of how to break free from limiting beliefs, reconnect with the wisdom of nature, reclaim your sovereignty, and harness our collective power to heal and co-create a world that benefits everyone.

We Are at a Crossroads

One path leads to further collapse, deeper division, and the eventual extinction of all we hold dear.

The other leads to evolution—to awakening, unity, and the co-creation of a world built on truth, freedom, and love.

This is not a time for passive hope. It is a time for active awakening.

To those who feel the call—to those who know, deep inside, that they came here for a reason—this book is for you.

The time is now.

Open your eyes.

Expand your mind.

And choose wisely.

1

Introducing Penny Kelly

MY FIRST INTRODUCTION to Penny Kelly was through her book *Robes*, which was published in 2005. I came across *Robes* seven or eight years ago and couldn't put it down. I was utterly absorbed. I even had my team read it, and we discussed it on our calls—it was that eye-opening. The book reinforced something a dear friend once told me: to truly evolve, we must unlearn much of what we've been taught and relearn in a way that aligns with a deeper, more natural flow of life. Needless to say, I became a fan.

What I admired most was how clearly Penny laid out a vision of reality, human consciousness, and the forces that shape our perceptions. She presented a compelling case for why, if we can reimagine our understanding of science, governance, education, finance, and medicine, we have the power to create a whole new world—literally. But as she wisely points out:

"We can't know where we're going if we don't know where we've been. And we won't know where we've been if we continue to ignore the way things work in our reality system. So, we need to take a long, clear, objective look at what is happening around us."

Penny encourages us to deeply examine the reality we've lived in for so long—to reflect on who we are, question our assumptions, and take full responsibility for our lives. Only by doing so can we navigate the changes ahead with clarity and purpose.

Now, here's where things get interesting. My friend and editor, Sandie Sedgbeer (who seems to know *everyone*), also knew Penny. When she suggested featuring Penny in the documentary *It's Time...* I had the same reaction as when Sandie first mentioned Synthia Andrews—pure excitement. But at the same time, I was a little insecure. A prolific author and highly respected teacher with a massive following, I doubted Penny would have the interest or time to be part of the film.

I couldn't have been more wrong. Not only was Penny interested, but she also generously offered her beautiful farmhouse in Michigan as a filming location. And so, with our production schedule in hand and a heart full of gratitude, my team and I made our way to the small town of Lawton, in my home state of Michigan, ready to capture Penny's wisdom on film.

Penny Kelly is vibrant, brilliant, and just the right amount of crazy—the kind of crazy I love having in my circle! She welcomed us with open arms, letting us take over her home for a few wintry days while we filmed. Her generosity and warmth left a lasting impression on me.

Meeting Penny Kelly wasn't just an item to check off my bucket list—it was an experience I'll carry with me forever. Her insights, her energy, and her presence have left a permanent mark on my journey, and for that, I'm deeply grateful.

A New Beginning
by Penny Kelly

"The medicine of the future depends as much on what we don't do as what we do."
—PENNY KELLY

One of the great myths of our time is that we evolved from apes into humans and that was the end of our evolution. Nothing could be more inaccurate. We are continuously evolving creatures from the moment of our creation until the moment we leave this reality system and step beyond.

The world we see around us is a result of the consciousness we hold. As we change, we change our world. Those changes are usually slow and incremental, but now and then there will be a paradigm shift—an overhaul of the entire system. We are in one of those times, and the current paradigm shift has been both invitation and threat, depending on your perspective. This shift is not the end of everything. It's a new beginning in which everything will be re-examined, re-designed, re-organized, and rebuilt.

In the same way that we put a variety of ingredients together to make a cake or ferment a yogurt, every civilization has about a dozen ingredients or areas of function that must work together to create a successful society. These "ingredients" are things like food, medicine, governance, education, science, etc. and each serves to preserve and protect the society. The food sector has to feed people; medicine's job is to heal people; education must teach them how to survive and cooperate; governance must devise rules for living together peacefully; science must continue researching and testing to improve life for all. We also have business, trade, technology, and financial systems that must evolve. Then there is religion, art, music, and dance. All of these sectors work together…and together they form a paradigm, which can be thought of as the infrastructure of life at a given point in time. You cannot change just one of those sectors without impacting or undermining the entire infrastructure.

World-building is big, exciting work! I wrote *The Revival* to help with that process. We are an amazing group of humans, here to enjoy life on a small planet. We are designed to evolve, but we have been conditioned to believe in limitation instead of expansion. We have been taught to believe that power exists outside of us, which leaves us helpless and often hopeless. This conditioning began with the advent of organized religion.

When religions or organizations tell you the real authority is outside the Self, you begin to look for answers and permissions everywhere but where they are. You stop trusting yourself. Eventually you believe you have no right to your own power. You become a victim of circumstance.

Individuals are not the only victims of organized religion. Whole sectors can also become victims. An example here is science and the persecution of scientists as organized religion began to restrict new knowledge in an attempt to prevent change. This caused a serious split between the two sectors. The result was the declaration by scientists that they would only allow *objective* observations to be considered as legitimate in their research. Anything *subjective* would be dismissed or ignored. However, individual consciousness is entirely subjective, and when you remove subjectivity, you remove people, their consciousness, their perspectives, ways of doing things, and their power! This was a huge setback for the evolution of humanity and the cause of what can now be seen as arrested development of the humans of Earth.

My goal in writing *The Revival* was to make us aware of what we are doing with our consciousness. It was to restore our lost power and remind people that *it is the nature of consciousness to create*.

If we want a new world, we must develop consciousness, reinstate our inner authority, and regain trust in ourselves. To do this we need a new way of seeing and thinking about the world. We must expand and deepen into a more cohesive understanding of our reality system and our place in it as we watch what is happening in real-time, everyday living. If we can grasp the hidden drivers behind unfolding events and learn to assess the short and long-term outcomes that are likely, we can begin to understand consciousness and take charge of the great power it holds.

The Revival presents a brief overview of how our culture has changed as people made new decisions and took steps in a particular direction. From a 40-thousand-foot view, I have tried to present the basics of each sector and what happens once it has flowered and begun to degenerate. What is the legacy of that sector, the seeds of its future, and how it is likely to affect or be affected by changes in other sectors.

At the end of each chapter, I provide a lengthy list of questions designed to help people understand the Self, who you are, why you think the way you do, and what belief systems you hold about that area of life. Many readers have been prodded into awakening by these questions. We are the ones creating this reality and until now, have not been very good at recognizing our power. Even now it is only beginning to be recognized that consciousness—either ours or someone else's, is the determiner of everything that happens in life.

The bottom line is that we must be willing to go inside and ask ourselves tough questions about our relationship with and contribution to each of these sectors. Only then can we rediscover our power and begin to build the world we want.

Agriculture, Food, Water, and Nutrition

Over the last few decades, many changes have occurred in the sector of agriculture, food and nutrition. The sudden mushrooming of big business and corporate jobs coaxed people away from the land and farms. I come from a farming, ranching, cattle-dealing family. Working the land, growing your own food, and all that this entails is hard work. What attracted people to corporate jobs was the notion that life would be easier, and in many ways, it was. However, this move into industry had severe impacts on how food is grown, on human health, animals and livestock, family and social relationships, money, art, science, and even the land itself.

Today, as successive generations are born and live further and further away from the soil, the health of our population has seriously deteriorated. As health deteriorates, society begins to disintegrate. We are now five generations away from the soil, and each generation has suffered another, more serious level of degeneration.

Our system of agriculture produces food for millions of people. But the legacy of *how* we are managing this system is a serious absence of nutrition. People are getting sick and beginning to degenerate at younger and younger ages. This is evident in the drastic change in the statistics of asthma, allergies, obesity, diabetes, cardiovascular disease, and early-onset cancer. Far too many people in their 40s—and even children—are struggling with cancer. This is not normal. Worse, we are now almost unable to reproduce and repopulate.

How Did We Get Here?

There are many answers. One is that we have disconnected ourselves from Mother Nature. Many of us have completely forgotten or never understood the living system of nature we are embedded in. Thus, we don't understand that the health problems plaguing us are caused by food that has no nutrition in it, soil that has not been renewed, and dead water that is often more destructive than constructive. The level of our ignorance has reached dangerous levels, and we can no longer afford to ignore the fact that nature is our backup system, not technology. High technology is wonderful, but if it fails, we will need Mother Nature as our backup system.

Every civilization must figure out what to eat in order to obtain the complete set of amino acids needed by humans. In the West, meat, milk, and eggs provide all the aminos needed. However, if the meat comes from animals raised in crowded animal pens without access to pasture and room to forage, it will have many nutritional deficiencies.

Animals, like humans, are wired for two things—pain or pleasure. When animals experience pleasure, they can absorb nutrition and thrive. Conversely, when they experience stress and pain, very little nutrition will be absorbed. The situation gets worse if our animals are highly stressed *and* not well-fed.

If the animals we eat do not get optimal nutrition, they will suffer the same kinds of degeneration that humans suffer. Cows on pasture will uptake plenty of calcium. Cows on corn and soy will not have access to the calcium they need and will uptake extra potassium from the corn they are fed. As a result, the quality of the meat will be poor. The burgers or steak you cook will shrink away to nothing and can be tough, tasteless, flavorless, and lacking in the nutrition we need to stay healthy. If cattle are being raised to feed us and they do not have access to grasses, herbs, and other nutrients found only in the fields, everyone loses.

There are similar problems in raising chickens on factory-produced feed without access to grass and the bugs that provide them with proteins. The result is that the chicken on your plate lacks aminos, omega factors, and other nutrients. Ditto for their eggs. Again, we end up as losers because it takes a lot of internal energy for the human body to process what we put into it. The body spends time, energy, and effort to find and extract nutrients that aren't there. It is like paying for groceries only to arrive home and find the grocery bags are empty.

We have an epidemic of nutritional deficiencies in the world today.

Some people take vitamins but often neglect to think about minerals and almost never consider amino acids. Yet these supplements are needed by the entire body/mind system. There are 29 major aminos, six major minerals, a dozen or so major vitamins, approximately 100 trace minerals, and a host of other important nutrients, all of which are necessary for a healthy body and a calm, clear mind.

Lack of nutrition greatly affects human emotions, mood, and behavior. Every amino acid, mineral, and vitamin contributes a little something to your consciousness and perception. For example, without enough of the amino acid histidine it is difficult to experience any kind of pleasure, including sexual pleasure. A lack of magnesium leaves you not wanting to be touched. Insufficient calcium leaves you depressed, sluggish, unable to sleep, think clearly, or think in a linear fashion. Without enough potassium, it is difficult to hold your focus in this reality. You begin to see things that others don't see. Then people say, "Oh, he's having a hallucination; he needs a drug. Put him in a hospital."

Let me say it again...the aminos, minerals, and vitamins the body needs are also needed to create a clear, calm, and powerful consciousness that is able to focus and knows what it wants. Without an optimal supply of nutrition, you won't have the full power of consciousness that should be at your fingertips.

I've already mentioned stress, but let's go a little deeper. The official name of stress is the *General Adaptation Syndrome*. Stress is not just a fantasy or a figment of your imagination. Stress triggers a series of physiological reactions in the body. It doesn't matter whether a tiger is chasing you, your boss is yelling at you, or your imagination is working overtime with some kind of worry; a common series of physical changes occurs regardless of what causes your stress.

This series of changes occurs in three stages. In Stage 1, *Alarm*, something triggers the start of the *fight-or-flight* response. Within seconds, the pituitary and adrenals produce adrenocorticotropic hormone (ACTH), cortisone, and cortisol bringing quick energy and a fast heartbeat. Digestion shuts down, blood pressure rises, and sugar from the liver pours into the bloodstream to give quick energy to muscles and the brain. Blood is withdrawn from your extremities and moved into the deep interior of the body to safeguard your organs. Blood-clotting factors pour into your bloodstream to slow down any blood loss in the event of an open wound, and as your blood withdraws and thickens, your blood vessels, arteries, and cardiovascular system shrink to obstruct blood flow, helping to prevent you from bleeding to death. Brain-generated endorphins (opiates) pour into the blood stream to dull perception and ease pain, and this entire sequence is in full operation within two minutes of the onset of stress.

Stage 2 is *Resistance*, and in this stage the fight or flight is on. More of the above chemicals are released, whatever has shut down stays shut down, and you rally intensely to defend the body. If stage two continues without sufficient nutrition for an extended period, it may lead to diarrhea, vomiting, bloating, weight gain due to the cortisol and cortisone, and dozens of other problems.

Of course, you can live with temporary stress, but if the stress goes on for more than two years, you enter Stage 3, *Exhaustion*, in which your resources are depleted, and the defense and immune system wear down. Without immediate relief and attention to healing, the body gives up and dies.

This stress response happens across the globe to millions of executives every Monday morning when they start their trek back to work, feeling stressed and anxious at being "back in the saddle again." And it all happens in just two minutes. Stage 2 of this syndrome is also widespread in our society, particularly in the West, leaving millions of people trapped in this harmful cycle with little understanding or knowledge of how to improve their situation.

Stress is a killer and a drastic wearing force. The body suffers greatly when the digestive system is shut down for lengthy periods, and you will be in danger of increased susceptibility to whatever genetic weakness runs in your family. To provide immediate relief, you need to begin supplying the body with four times more nutrition than usual for an extended period of time.

Because our food system has been severely compromised, many rely on supplements to provide the missing nutrients. This is helpful, but it is more important to make sure that we renew the soils our food is grown in. Plants are intelligent living systems that produce valuable co-factors that are missing from factory foods and even some supplements.

Foods such as microgreens, fruits, vegetables, herbs, and healthy, happy, grass-fed meat sources are critical to maintaining good health. Microgreens, which are great in smoothies, have 400-800 times more nutrients than the same plant would have if left to mature fully. Many foods are destroyed by cooking, especially over-cooking. Raw foods are more nutritious than cooked foods because their proteins have not been denatured by heat. If we want to be healthy, we have to expand awareness of all these factors and pay closer attention to what we put in the body.

Before closing these comments on the problems in the agriculture sector, it is important to mention water. Water is the most basic form of medicine we know. It is essential for life and for maintaining excellent health. Many people have experienced healing from various diseases simply by consuming *living* water. While we often have easy access to a lot of water, much of it is *dead* water. The molecules in living water have a left-hand spin, which is centripetal, very magnetic, and is form-building. Dead water has molecules with a right-hand spin, which is very centrifugal, anti-magnetic, and disintegrates form.

When water is drawn out of the earth before it is *mature*, i.e., before it rises naturally to the surface, it will be dead water because it has not gone through several critical processes on its way from deep in the earth to the surface. Even if it has gone through those processes, when we capture it in pipes and holding tanks where it sits, warms, and is not allowed to move, it will lose its left-hand spin and revert to being dead water. Millions of people are drinking dead water, which is very hard on the body.

While the sectors of life in a paradigm may seem distinct and independent, they are not. Their functions and legacies are interconnected. Each either promotes life or furthers the disconnect between body and mind. Here is a brief look at a few more examples.

Religion

Religion has proven to be a formidable barrier to a healthy, balanced consciousness. Many of us have been taught to believe in an all-powerful authority that exists outside the self. This mythical authority is always watching, judging, and threatening to send us to hell. We have not yet been able to put ourselves back in charge of our consciousness again.

Religion has also been extremely successful in introducing guilt for not living a "godly" life defined by priests, and shame for having a human body. When people think of their bodies as unclean, as shameful, as some useless temporary structure they are caught in, they are seldom able to reach the peaks of genius, wisdom, joy, power, and grace that are their birthright. Body and mind become two weirdly separate things with no real connection. The result is a failure to use our intuition and its treasured, truthful responses to life and the demand for clear, steady decision-making. We also fail to use our consciousness to heal the body. This is tragic because the result is a fractured population in which people treat their bodies as either irrelevant or as a machine! We humans are living, thinking, and feeling beings that are overflowing with creativity and potential. We are dynamically evolving and meant to evolve even further. Consciousness is our best tool for doing so.

Education

I was an educational consultant for eighteen years, working with schools and corporations. I specialized in Accelerated and Brain-Compatible Teaching and Learning. However, I left because the people running this sector did not want to make any changes. I would run seminars, talk about the brain, brain-compatible learning, and how we could greatly enhance child development, and school principals would ask, "What does the brain have to do with learning?" I was stunned. All I could say was, "Wow, the brain has *everything* to do with education."

How does the brain work? How does perception work? What is consciousness? And cognition? What about the development of the individual? There is so much that we have yet to learn! What could be more basic and useful than understanding how the body/mind system works and then nurturing each individual to his or her highest possibilities?

Few people know that when you truly grasp something new, you change at a deep level, and this includes a change in your DNA! The body is our main channel for learning, especially when we are young. However, in schools and colleges across the land, children are tucked into classrooms and desks all day where they are expected to sit quietly, not speak unless spoken to, and conform to strict rules. They are limited to working with paper and pencils, taught many things they will never find useful, tested to see how well they have memorized what the teacher was teaching, and given grades that convey deep competition and a label that often stigmatizes them for life. The legacy of this system is that children are limited to knowing how to use a pencil and paper but very little about how the real world works. They are conditioned to stop thinking for themselves and accept what someone tells them to think. They are "graded" as if they were eggs or apples, and they become highly competitive.

Humans learn by copying. This is especially true of children. They are like little monkeys in this regard because it's the fastest and most efficient way to learn. Yet copying is forbidden in schools. What is the result? It is a complete absence of cooperation, and later in life it is the tragic waste of time, energy, and intelligence as those with creative ideas often work alone because they fear someone will copy them and steal their idea.

Many teachers are leaving the profession because they no longer find it fulfilling. When I was working in educational consulting, research showed that teachers spent only about eleven minutes of each hour actually teaching. The rest of the time was spent managing the children—directing, guiding, getting them to form lines to go to the bathroom, putting on or taking off coats or boots, corralling them to go to lunch or back to the classroom, and disciplining them. Teachers today have little opportunity to share their passion and enthusiasm for the subjects they love. They have no autonomy and must teach only what they are told to teach. This often leads to frustration and disengagement, and children are sensitive enough to pick up on it. Do we want our children to copy this?

One of the first things we should teach children is survival. That's primary. Reading, writing, arithmetic, science, technology, languages, history, and geography come later because the need to learn to manage oneself in the face of Mother Nature is far greater.

We should also be teaching children about consciousness and how to manage theirs. Alpha, beta, theta, delta, high beta, gamma… each frequency state allows for different kinds of perception and different responses to information. Kids want to know who they are and how their system works so they can work with it to become their true self, but they're not given an opportunity. Instead, they are told who they are. As we mature and enter the later stages of adult development, we need to understand the effect that different levels and states of consciousness have on us so we can flower as enlightened beings. Brain-compatible learning encourages the development of the whole person, and an entirely new educational system is needed for that kind of development.

Closing Thoughts About Legacies

The above is a small snapshot from *The Revival*. Since I wrote the book, the grip of religion has begun to loosen as more and more corruption has been uncovered. The education sector is very efficient at breaking down our ability to make connections and figure things out. Is it surprising that more and more parents refuse to send their children to school? Homeschooling, which is already big in the United States, will grow by leaps and bounds over the next five to ten years.

Governance is also struggling with corruption, as is medicine, which is more focused on profit than on healing and preventing disease. One of the primary problems with the medicine of today is that it's populated by specialists. We have the ear, nose and throat guy, the heart guy, the podiatrist, psychiatrist, dentist, and others. They're all specialists. Unfortunately, when we begin to specialize, we become millions of Humpy Dumpty characters. Who will put us back together again? We need a paradigm change in terms of understanding ourselves as beings on Planet Earth!

A New Way of Seeing Ourselves and Our Possibilities

A paradigm change always includes seeing ourselves with new eyes and embracing ideas we couldn't even imagine before. What possibilities await us if we are able to change course and carve a new pathway? Can we come together in meaningful conversations, assess the reality we have been living in for many years, take responsibility for our lives, and start co-creating anew?

To do this, we must understand and acknowledge that we can no longer look at change as if we are innocent bystanders caught in the storm. If we want to improve our lives in a practical way, if we want to thrive, not just survive, we need to become new humans. This means that we must start to think differently, understand the nature of reality, and clearly align ourselves with what we are willing to support. We've each had input into the present paradigm and cannot change it without deeply assessing who we are and what we want our lives to be. In short, we cannot create a new world with an old consciousness. We need to expand and evolve!

Whenever I talk about expanding our consciousness, people nod in agreement. However, in my experience, few truly understand what this means or the depth of change that accompanies this expansion.

First, expanding consciousness is something that we can all do. Expanding consciousness means not limiting perception to local time and space. It means being intuitive, opening your intelligence, and broadening your outlook. Expanding consciousness results in an understanding of what is visible as well as what is hidden and seeing why people do what they do. It includes being able to read Mother Nature, and to use your power to make your life and the world a better place. Although many people have never thought about these things, they are a natural part of the toolkit that we all have. It's all in the body/mind.

Each of us is a collection of frequencies and a unique perceiver of the frequencies surrounding us. We all have a frequency signature, but it is not set in stone and DNA responds to changing frequencies. For example, let's say you wanted to hypnotize somebody with multiple personality disorder (MPD). If you took a DNA sample while they were in one personality and then hypnotized them to move into another personality, you would find that their second DNA sample would be different. That's how flexible DNA is. Our bodies are dynamic. As our perception changes, our chemistry and hormones change, and since our hormones manage all our responses, our reactions change.

Our frequency cycles naturally over the course of each day as it moves through beta, alpha, theta, and delta, and each of these states of frequency allows for a differing kind of activity in the mind. For example, beta is a reality builder. Alpha is for reflecting and assessing what you just built. Theta is for coming up with new, intuitive, and more refined aspects of your reality. And delta is for healing and restoring yourself after all the above work. The bottom line: *When you change your frequency, you change your consciousness.*

Consciousness is a tool that we point at different objects and actions to stay informed of what is happening around us. When we begin to point our consciousness or awareness at places that have a higher frequency, our DNA, which is a set of frequency receivers changes to accommodate us. The greater the range of energy you can hold and allow to flow freely through you, the more your consciousness will expand.

We have this magnificent brain whose primary job is to help our body respond appropriately to the ocean of frequencies in which we live, and to be a tool by which we explore those frequencies and the possibilities within them. To do so is literally to explore the possibilities of life and the self.

The human brain is a receiver and transmitter that always takes in an astounding amount of information, helping us to navigate, create, and respond to reality. People say, "Oh, but we're only using 10% of our brain," as if we're not using the other 90%. Nothing could be further from the truth! That other 90% is tuned into the rest of the cosmos and what is going on non-locally. When you learn how to manage your brainwave frequencies, you can move deliberately into various frequency ranges and control the kind of information available to you. This is something we could be teaching children from the ground up because consciousness is where our power is.

This is just the barest outline of frequencies and how they express themselves in our lives, but when you study them, they are complex, elegant, and intimately related to thoughts, feelings, and behavior. If we want to uncover our full potential as humans and build a new world, we need to understand consciousness, how it works, and what affects it.

How To Change Your Frequency

There are several ways of changing your frequency or keeping it at one level or another. My personal preference is breathwork, which is extremely powerful. Another way is to be conscious of where you're placing your attention. Watching a lot of TV, especially crime programs, can quickly lower your frequency, as can watching the news, so it's important to balance bad news or negative programming with good news. Likewise, failing to do your personal root work will keep your frequency low. Root work is self-inquiry, getting to the root of biases and fears.

As mentioned earlier, it's all in the body/mind. Listening to uplifting music, something as silly as watching cat videos and laughing until you almost cry, connecting with others, meditation, practicing kindness, compassion, empathy, and opening your heart to others will all raise your frequency. For most people, meditation is helpful, but elevating consciousness begins much more often with doing something that makes you feel good about yourself. The entire frequency matrix of the body is the foundation from which consciousness arises. Consciousness is the *feeling* aspect of energy. Energy is the *motion* of consciousness. They are two sides of one coin. The more feelings you allow yourself to feel, the more your consciousness will expand and this always changes your frequency.

Energy and the Future of Medicine

The medicine of the future will be energy medicine. The body is a collection of frequencies that form plasmas. A plasma is a pattern of relationships formed by spiraling electric currents, the electromagnetic fields that surround those currents, and the particles they create. Saying it another way…A plasma is the underlying pattern of energies and particles that form all matter, including the body. As we come to understand frequencies and their patterns, we will learn how to adjust or change these frequencies to heal or correct many things.

The medicine of the future will be as much about what we *don't* do as what we *do*. It will be based on the understanding that the body is a result of the energy pattern underlying the physical self. If this energy is not coherent or has been corrupted, just like a file on a CD or your computer, it can lead to dysfunctions in your body. Diseases and problems appear when the body's messaging system is corrupted. Instead of treating just one area of the body, future medicine will address the entire energy system. This will be done using frequencies of light, energy, sound, Mother Nature, herbs, and high-density nutritious food, all of which can have a transformative effect on the body's frequency pattern and overall well-being.

Energy medicine based on a whole new understanding of the human body/mind system and the nature of reality is the way of the future. Although we are close to this kind of medicine, we aren't there yet. In the meantime, it's critical to understand that what we're dealing with now is not so much a medical system that has gone wrong, it is that we have outgrown the paradigm that we were in. The science has changed, the technology has changed, the information has changed, everything is changing.

We often talk about wanting a better life, dreaming of a world where peace prevails, life is fulfilling, and everyone has everything they need. We all want to care for ourselves in ways that prevent degeneration and disability so we can enjoy every moment of life until the very end. However, we rarely consider that achieving a better life may involve enduring the breakdown of the old world before we can reach the new one. We seldom think about the kind of humans we would need to become in order to create and maintain a new paradigm.

The paradigm we are moving into is one in which the evolution of consciousness is a steady theme that will help us navigate the paradigm shift. We must have a vision of what we could create, or we won't be able to hang on while everything is changing. It's important to remember that while it may look, feel, and sound like everything is falling apart, it's not. Old paradigms do disintegrate, but if you're paying attention, you will soon see the threads of the new one coming together as we develop new ways of governing, educating, feeding ourselves, and thinking about business, technology, art, and science.

It's a painful process when everything changes too quickly or we are not prepared, but it's part of the evolutionary unfolding of civilization that will carry us from the third dimension to the fourth and the fifth. This means stepping into higher frequency ranges and dropping some of the lower frequencies. As these changes occur and the old systems crumble, it's natural to feel anxious. But there is no need; it's a normal part of the process. Without change and renewal, we would eventually disintegrate and come to nothing. It's either survive and thrive…or disintegrate and die.

When I look to the future, I see no trace of humanity taking the latter path. We are a species busy with a massive collective awakening. I see humanity reviving, thriving, and evolving.

It's time to fully embrace who we are and how we want our lives to be as we reinvent the world for ourselves, our children, and all who will come after them.

It's time to write a new story for humanity, to create a new paradigm that heals and is good for all.

PENNY KELLY is an author, teacher, publisher, consultant, Naturopathic physician, and researcher of the brain, intelligence, intuition, cognition, energy and consciousness. She holds a degree in Humanistic Studies from Wayne State University, a degree in Naturopathic Medicine from Clayton College of Natural Health. She spent 15 years working with biophysicist Dr. Wm. Levengood, studying materials from crop circles, animal mutilations, and ET landing sites, as well as researching plasma, energy, and consciousness.

Penny was involved in starting Community Gardening in Kalamazoo and Battle Creek, MI through grants from the Kellogg Foundation, and was a member of the Tipping Point Network whose focus is sustainability in all sectors of life. She maintains a worldwide counseling and coaching practice, teaches a half-dozen courses in *Developing Intuition—The Gift of Consciousness*, as well as courses in *Organic Gardening*, and *Getting Well Again Naturally*. She produces regular videos for Patreon, YouTube, and BitChute, and travels widely to speak and teach.

Penny is the author of multiple books including 4 volumes of *Consciousness and Energy*; *The Elves of Lily Hill Farm: A Partnership with Nature*; *Robes: A Book of Coming Changes*; *The Evolving Human: A True Story of Awakened Kundalini*; *Getting Well Again From The Soil To The Stomach*, and *The Revival—A Path to A New Earth /New Human*.

www.pennykelly.com

Gail's Conscious Living Challenge:
Grow Something.
Question Everything.

Penny's chapter is packed with so much insight—how can I possibly summarize it all? It reminds me of the many myths I grew up hearing, like ingesting mercury for skin diseases and constipation, bloodletting being considered healthy, or even smoking as a weight-loss strategy. Looking back, it's almost unbelievable that these ideas were once widely accepted. What are some myths you've heard that have since been debunked?

What I love most about Penny's perspective is how she emphasizes the interconnectedness of the body and the importance of daily self-care. One of the simplest yet most powerful things we can do for ourselves is to grow our own food. After meeting Penny, I started growing microgreens at home and was amazed at how nutrient-dense they are. So, here's my challenge: grow *one* thing you can eat. Microgreens are a great place to start—they're easy, fun to watch grow, and full of life-giving nutrients. You can even find beginner-friendly kits online.

Penny also invites us to think critically about our health. When something feels off in your body, step back and ask yourself: *What has changed in my life recently?* Not every symptom needs an immediate medical intervention—sometimes, the answer lies in our lifestyle, environment, trauma, or even our mindset.

Stress, grief, accidents, and unresolved trauma all affect the body—and sometimes those effects don't show up until long after the original incident. For example, researchers at the University of Michigan found that childhood adversity and trauma can increase the risk of tooth loss later in life.[1] Grief—such as the death of a loved one—can trigger a cascade of physical symptoms, from changes in appetite and sleep to aches, pains, and even a weakened immune system, which may lead to illness or more serious health issues.[2]

I'll share a quick example: a friend of mine recently experienced sudden swelling around his nose and eyes. His doctors immediately recommended tubes in his eyes, but something didn't sit right. He had just recovered from a rough winter flu and had been taking prednisone, antibiotics, and sleep aids. That combination alone could have triggered unexpected side effects. It's a reminder that we must look beyond the surface and consider the bigger picture—what's happening holistically in our lives and our bodies?

I also want to challenge you to rethink hydration. Sounds strange, right? But could *too much* water be contributing to some of your health issues? I used to drink a gallon a day and needed loads of supplements just to keep up with the minerals I was flushing out. Clear urine, which many people think is a sign of good hydration, is actually a sign your body isn't retaining water properly. Proper hydration means your body is using water efficiently—to sweep out toxins, support your cells, and maintain balance. Urine should have some color—not dark orange or brown (a sign of dehydration), but also not completely clear.

Before the bottled water boom, people drank when they were thirsty. Now, many of us have overridden that natural signal by constantly drinking excessive amounts of water. The body adapts to this overflow by evacuating more often, and that becomes the new normal. It's worth rethinking how we approach hydration—listen to your body, and don't assume more is always better. For more surprising facts about hydration, read my article on The Mystery of Hydration.[3]

Ultimately, I challenge you to think for yourself. Connect the dots. Use common sense. Don't be afraid to question what you've been told about your body and your health. When something feels off, ask: *Could food be my medicine?* Too often, we reach for supplements or prescriptions without questioning their source, quality, or necessity and without considering the healing potential of real, whole foods. Yes, our soils are depleted, and food isn't what it once was—but food is still foundational to our well-being.

If you think your body needs more magnesium, start by eating magnesium-rich foods instead of relying on a supplement whose source, energy, or ingredients you can't trace.

And finally, reduce your stress. As Penny points out, stress inhibits your body's ability to absorb nutrients. Make time—even if it's just once a week—to slow down. Eat with presence and gratitude. Avoid eating while rushing, multitasking, or stressing out. And if you can, ground yourself: put your feet on the earth or your hands in the soil. Your nervous system will thank you. I'll leave you with a few reminders from two of my favorite authors:

> *"When you change the way you see things, the things you see will change."* — WAYNE DYER

> *"Chaos is necessary—it's the bridge between one transformation and another."* — BRUCE LIPTON

So, embrace change, question everything, and take small daily steps that bring you closer to a healthier, more conscious way of living. You have more power than you realize.

1. *https://news.umich.edu/childhood-trauma-tied-to-tooth-loss-later-in-life/*
2. *https://www.helpguide.org/mental-health/grief/bereavement-grieving-the-death-of-a-loved-one*
3. *https://harmonicegg.com/the-mystery-of-hydration-waters-energy-and-its-impact-on-wellness/*

2

Introducing
Synthia Andrews, N.D.

I HAD RECEIVED a copy of Synthia Andrew's book, *Subtle Energy Work*, from a friend. It was a page-turner for me, and when we were looking to cast the professionals for my documentary, *It's Time*…, Sandie Sedgbeer, the scriptwriter, suggested we consider Synthia. I was 100% on board. I was so nervous to meet Synthia and even more anxious that she would not like the documentary concept and would say NO. She did not. She said YES and the rest is history.

In my estimation, Synthia's profound understanding of energy and how to work with it puts her in a class of her own. Working with her on the film was an absolute pleasure, and I hope we have a long friendship.

Subtle Energy Work: The Language of the Heart
by Synthia Andrews, N.D.

Overview

We are living in unprecedented times; a thought we hear repeatedly as our paradigm shifts and accelerated change carries us into the unknown. Ancient prophecies of the Maya predicted this period as a time when the old breaks down to make way for the new. We see this today in the dismantling of the current belief systems, religions, governments, technology, science, and social and personal structures while Earth herself is undergoing geological upheaval and climate change. Prophecy suggests that the current chaos is one of purification, in which old patterns and structures that no longer work are brought into alignment with the energy of expanded awareness.

We can consider this process an evolutionary bottleneck in which the old becomes so large it collapses under its own weight, forcing us into unchartered territory. What happens on the other side of the bottleneck, what the future holds, is not accidental. How each of us acts and what we bring to the table during the challenge of collapse is creating the quality of our future. The heroes we invest in to save us are an illusion. According to the Maya, we are the ones we are looking for. Each of us must find the hero within.

Purification is the cleansing of a mindset that has poisoned the Earth and put obstacles in the path of spiritual realization for the purpose of control, power, and greed. The question becomes, what inner growth is required for us to navigate the perils of these times? As we face personal loss and chaos, we discover the only way through is to align with higher principles of love, respect, and compassion. As a culture, we've been conditioned into division, manipulated into believing there is an us and them because as long as we fight each other, we're easily manipulated while those who do the manipulation grow richer. Overriding deception requires the discernment of wisdom, which resides within the heart.

Why Now?

Many ask, why is this paradigm shift happening now? Perhaps we've exhausted the direction our current mindset can take us. Or maybe it's because we're ready; enough people are choosing love, kindness, and respect to produce the hundredth monkey effect that initiates change. Perhaps Earth's movement through the universe has shifted into a new alignment and the energy coming in is stimulating new thoughts. However, why this is happening now might not be as important as how we respond.

Einstein said that we can't solve today's problems using the same thinking that created them. Thinking differently requires perceiving from a new vantage point. We may need to listen to people we disagree with, exchange ideas with cultures we don't understand, and, most importantly, listen to Earth and nature.

In the chaos of the bottleneck, communication is one of our biggest challenges. Despite the multitude of communication tools and the capability to talk to anyone, anywhere on the planet, at any time, our ability to connect more deeply has been impaired. Words mean different things to different people. They are coded in layers that reflect each person's beliefs, trauma, and social engineering.

Tiokasin Ghosthorse, a Lakota Sioux man and host of First Voices radio, says we can't wake up using the same language that put us to sleep. He declares that the language that will wake us up is the language of the Heart, the place within where truth resides.

The heart knows what is worth saving and what must be let go of. Yet listening to the heart is a skill we've largely forgotten. Our inner truth has been overlaid with survival fear. To hear the heart, we need to find our center, the place where we know we are powerful, spiritual beings who stand for something larger than personal gain. There is a bigger design than we can see; when we pay attention to the heart, we can feel it.

The Language of the Heart

The language of the heart is that of subtle energy, of listening to and feeling the information coming to us through the ambiance. Subtle energy awareness requires whole-body listening; paying attention to how our skin responds, how our muscles tighten, what our gut instincts say, and to our intuition as we engage the seen and unseen aspects of life. The flow of energy, like the mycelium of mushrooms, is the connective tissue of the planet. What is our body telling us about the world around us?

Already, consensual reality has broken down. We can't trust information found on social media, the internet, or commercial television. People see the same event and perceive different facts. With AI in the picture, how do we know what is true and what is manufactured? While energy awareness is one aspect of discernment, self-knowledge is the other. Almost every spiritual and philosophical tradition extolls us to 'Know Thyself.' This is because we perceive through the lens of our personal bias.

To see past our conditioning, we must understand how our experiences and wounds have shaped us. While energy awareness reveals truth, sometimes the truth it reveals is where our pain has limited our thinking and directed our perceptions. The resultant wound becomes a receptor site that is easily manipulated. As Voltaire allegedly said, "Anyone who can make you believe absurdities can make you commit atrocities."

Everyone intuitively knows the language of energy. We're born understanding this language, wired to negotiate the energy terrain of life. Every person in every nation, every animal, plant, tree, and Earth herself communicates through energy. In the process of socialization, we've simply forgotten how. Navigating the purification underway requires that we remember.

The Subtle Energy Paradigm

It's human nature to want to create the future in the image of the past. However, the nature of a paradigm shift is outside of what already exists. It's something new, and if we already know what it is, it isn't a paradigm change.

Einstein's groundbreaking equation $E=MC^2$ (energy equals matter times the speed of light squared) was a scientific paradigm shift in the 20th century. The equation reveals that energy and matter are different aspects of the same substance, separated only by their rate of vibration. We can say that energy and matter live in a perpetual dance of transformation: energy is entrained in matter, and matter is released back to energy. This dance of nature creates the world we know—all we see, feel, hear, taste, touch, sense, and measure with our technology.

Energy is a carrier wave of information in the form of vibration, or frequency. All life forms and objects emit radiation of specific, defining frequency called a signature frequency. NASA uses signature frequencies to identify the gases in the atmosphere of planets. Imagine living within a sea of energy of varying frequencies, each a packet of information about the world around us, a medium we live within that relates us to everything else.

Some of the information subtle energy transmits forms the templates that organize matter into specific form. Cymatics, developed in the early 20th century by the Swiss physician and natural scientist, Dr. Hans Jenny, demonstrates this organizing principle. Jenny showed how sound frequency vibrates sand into different shapes and forms. When the frequency of the sound changes, the geometric pattern created in the sand changes.[1]

Jenny speculated that our three-dimensional reality is constructed and maintained through the presence of different frequencies. While his demonstration was based on sound, the principle can be applied to frequencies emitted by colored lights, emotions, and even thoughts as every aspect of physicality emits a signature frequency. An EKG (electrocardiogram), for example, measures the frequency of the heart and an EEG (electroencephalogram) measures the frequency of the brain.

Masaru Emoto, a Japanese scientist, believed that consciousness can change the molecular structure of matter. His experiments provide a visual demonstration of how thoughts affect the crystalline structure of water, presented in his best-selling book, *The Messages in Water*. In his experiments, Emoto had groups of people focus on water with either positive or negative thoughts while the water was freezing. He then took pictures of the crystalline structures that formed. The patterns produced through negative intents were disorganized. When the same people focused on the freezing water with loving, coherent, positive thoughts, the crystalline structure formed symmetrical patterns.[2]

While we don't have the technology yet to measure subtle energy, these experiments demonstrate how subtle energy vibrations might affect matter. The construct is similar to the scientific description of dark energy and dark matter. Astrophysicists believe dark energy and dark matter comprise 95% of the universe, yet they cannot be seen, measured, or quantified and are only known through their effect. They are believed to be the scaffolding for the remaining 5% of the universe, the physical matter and energy we can measure. The description of dark energy and matter sounds surprisingly like the subtle energy that mystics have described for centuries.

Feeling into the energy ambiance reveals our relationship to the rest of creation, the animate and inanimate, the deeper parts of ourselves, and the seen and unseen parts of the universe. It teaches us that we are not alone and not separate; we are part of an interlocking whole.

Subtle Energy and Consciousness

Subtle energy is not energy as understood by physics. It is life force, an organizing, animating principle, and a carrier wave of information. Light is thought to be the most physical expression of subtle energy. The grandfather of quantum physics, David Bohm, called matter 'frozen light' and referred to light as the building block of matter. He said, "All matter is a condensation of light into patterns moving back and forth at average speeds which are less than the speed of light."[3] It's interesting that spiritual traditions say the same. According to Paramahansa Yogananda, "Light came first, and constitutes the essential structure of matter."[4] Light is often depicted as the source of inspiration, wisdom, and divine action.

If light is the first organizing principle of matter, then how it produces the universe is essentially holographic. We see holograms so often in images like three-dimensional key fobs or sculptures of heads with eyes that follow us as we move that we've lost appreciation of what they actually are. Holograms are created with crisscrossing beams of focused lasers that produce interference patterns from which three-dimensional images are structured. There are two things that are especially unique in the holographic images that are created. First, when a holographic image is torn in half, instead of creating two halves of the image, you end up with two pieces that each contain the entire image encoded within them. No matter how many times the hologram is torn, each fragment will still hold the complete image. Essentially, this means that the information from the whole hologram exists in every piece. In other words, each fragment contains the entirety of the image.

Second, while each piece of the torn hologram holds the complete image, it does so from the perspective of its original position in the hologram. As a result, each individual piece recreates the entire holographic image from its own viewpoint. While the whole image exists in each fragment, every angle is necessary to fully perceive it. Holography has redefined how scientists understand the natural world. Neuroscientists now believe that the brain codes information holographically in crisscrossing neural network patterns. Our memories, therefore, are not held in a specific section of tissue but in electric patterns. Consciousness itself is also considered holographic, as is the universe.[5]

If consciousness is holographic, each of us has access to the whole. More importantly, each of us creates the hologram by adding our unique perspective. The mosaic of what is produced is beyond what we can envision from one vantage point. To access the whole, we must expand out of our personal vantage point and let go of the importance we place on our personal frame of reference.

Holographic consciousness implies that the universe evolves with each piece of new information brought by the individual parts. Each of us, then, is directing evolution. As we go through this transition time, what contribution are we making through our feelings, thoughts, and actions in creating the future? What do we want to broadcast through our presence? We can continue to promote the current paradigm of self-importance, power, competition and duality or vision something better by being something better.

The fact is, we are not here at this time by accident. We were born for this moment, born to participate in this transformation. So, let's take the leap into greater awareness; let's expand beyond what we know with love, kindness, and compassion. Let's contribute the best of who we are to the future.

Experiencing Subtle Energy

Our body-mind is the instrument through which we experience and explore the energetic ambiance we live within. Our body is equipped with all the senses and extensions of the senses needed to fully engage this level of reality. We are biologically wired for every experience we have. We can't experience anything we're not designed to experience. We can't physically see frequencies of light outside the visible light spectrum or physically hear frequencies outside the design of our ears. But we can activate energy senses that do. Every far-out experience we've had only happened because we are designed for it. Either that, or we are stark raving mad. (But there are too many people having experiences for that to be true.) We've simply been taught that the energetic information we receive through our body-mind isn't valuable; that it's delusional and should be dismissed.

Since our bodies are wired to receive energy information, energy awareness begins with body awareness, paying attention to what's happening inside our body while simultaneously noticing the external world. We receive energy information through a series of energy structures that process it and turn it into emotions, feelings, body sensations, gut instincts, intuition, and inspired thoughts that create our perceptions. We can think of these body events as the vocabulary of our energy language. As we learn the language and pay attention to the information being received, we become aware of our relationship to everything around us, the plants, animals, and all the seen and unseen aspects of this reality.

Energy senses are derived from the aura, a biophysical radiation around the body, the chakras, energy processing centers, and the meridians, which are channels of life force that maintain the energy-to-physical template of the body. Frequencies in the ambiance are received in the aura and transmitted into the chakras where they are translated into the physical vocabulary of the energy language. The ability to hear this language is augmented by being centered, and listening to how the heart responds to what the body is feeling.

The exchange of information with the ambiance is a two-way street. We take in information, process it through our energy structures, subject it to our own lens of belief, and then project the result back out through the same pathway. In this way, we demonstrate our state of consciousness through our presence, the most powerful force we have. Without doing or saying anything, our presence broadcasts the deepest parts of who we are and what we value, impacting the world around us.

Like attracts like, and the frequencies we broadcast attract the frequencies we encounter. It's like social media. When we click on something we like, the algorithm brings our feed 100 more things that reflect the same viewpoint so that we become surrounded by our own perspective. In short, whatever we put into the world with our thoughts, emotions, and actions is what we attract until our picture of reality reflects our belief even more strongly. To become free, we must break through the patterns and bias based on our past experiences, both comfortable and uncomfortable.

In the quest to 'Know Thyself,' energy awareness can help break old conditioning. The patterns of our experiences are contained within our energy field, similarly to how they are contained in the neuro networks in our brain. They are the energetic imprints of our memories. Because the patterns direct how our energy is processed, they constrain and direct the flow of our energy. People stuck in specific patterns limit their ability to grow and have new experiences free of the bias of previous events.

Here are two examples. The first is someone stuck in survival mode. Imagine someone running out in front of a bus. Immediately, they experience fear and have the thought 'I'm going to die.' The fear of not surviving is generated in the root chakra and flows through the bladder and kidney meridian. As these energy structures receive an influx of energy, they light up, creating a pattern in the person's energy field. While the pattern is essential to mobilize the energy to attain safety, afterward, if the emotion of fear and thought of death is not processed, it solidifies in the energy field, and the person becomes stuck in survival thinking. The structure is held in place through the vibration of their initial fear, which becomes a charge in their energy field that is an attractive force for future events and the bias that directs their perceptions.

In a second example, imagine something powerfully positive such as the birth of a child, falling in love, or creating something beautiful. The activated energy structures might be the heart and crown, which fill the heart meridian and light the entire system. This pattern becomes a resource in the energy field that helps us expand our awareness and can be used to counter feelings of self-doubt or to overcome criticism. Whenever we feel left out, forgotten, or otherwise unseen, we can use the elevation of this pattern to lift up and bring in a higher frequency.

In the first situation, if the fear is processed, the energy gradually recedes from the pattern, and no longer holds a charge. The experience then provides the opportunity for growth through a deeper exploration of the fear activated when the bus approached—perhaps through delving into the fear of death, or what happens after death, and so on. Processing creates patterns geared toward growth, rather than limitation.

We become aware of our patterns by paying attention to what is happening in our body when we encounter situations that trigger our anger, fear, guilt or other limiting patterns whose functional aspect is long past. What muscles are tightening, and what chakras are drawing our attention? Track the energy into the key area of tension, then let the tension build while noticing your thoughts, feelings, and memories. Then breathe light into the area and exhale the tension out of your body. Sounds easy? It is. And it's effective when applied with practice and commitment.

The polarization of society is a survival pattern stuck in self-importance. We see ourselves as the only intelligent species on the planet and even in the universe. We limit our ability to experience a greater reality by separating ourselves from it and judging it as being less than we are. But judgment is the source of separation and separation is one of the things we are overcoming in the purification underway.

SUBTLE ENERGY WORK:
THE LANGUAGE OF THE HEART

Engaging Subtle Energy

Where we put our attention is where our energy flows and determines what we attract into our lives. In today's world, what we put out is coming back to us very quickly and with greater force than in the past. We need to consciously use the energy tools of attention and intention to negotiate the terrain. Energy follows the mind. Attention without intention creates unintended consequences.

Powerful, heart-centered intentions encompass our passion and spiritual beliefs. They are rooted in what we value and where our principles lie. They direct our attention so that our hearts, minds, and actions are aligned. The resultant integrity creates through choice rather than conditioning. Since the future is born out of the decisions of the present, the time to wake up to the future we want to create is now.

Medicine in Transition

In the chaos of these changing times, it's no surprise the world is in the midst of a medical crisis. The problem has many levels and layers, and greed has certainly played a role. How resources are allocated, who receives medical care, the influence of pharmaceutical empires, and the control insurance companies have over diagnostics, treatments, and medications are based on money and profit. When an insurance company can deny a doctor's prescription in order to improve profits, there's a fundamental problem in the system. In all instances, the equation is simple: shareholder profits are more important than people's lives.

Health is impacted by sedentary lifestyles, processed foods, contaminated food and water, and, of course, toxins. When we poison the planet, we poison ourselves. However, if there were one root cause of all sickness, it would be separation from nature. The cells in our body are harmonized to the frequencies of nature and the health effects of being in nature, such as the reduction of stress and elevation of mood, are well researched. Simply listening to birdsong is shown to immediately and significantly improve anxiety.[6] Conversely, the frequencies of technical devices are shown in multiple studies to disrupt cellular health.[7] The more estranged we are from nature, the more susceptible we are to illness.

The amount of time we spend with technology dulls us to the natural world and separates us from our inner self and power. It separates us from the reality that everything that sustains us—food, air, water, even everything we know—comes from nature. Every field of science studies a different aspect of the natural world; chemistry, physics, astrophysics, geometry, and biology are all derived from the study of nature. Every technological advancement comes from a deeper understanding of the laws that govern the natural world, and yet we treat the planet as a dumpster, with no respect or understanding of our dependency.

Energetically, we are intricately linked with the energy structures of Earth. We truly can't be separated. Our aura is part of the aura of Earth, our chakras relate to Earth's energy vortices, our meridians are woven into the channels of life force. Ancient people understood this relationship. The pyramids of the Maya and Egyptians and the megalithic sites of England, Europe, and the Americas were built in alignment with Earth energy. The Maya utilized energy alignments to magnify the intention of their buildings and society. Asian cities were designed with Feng Shui to synergize with natural flow. In organic cultures, the interlocking connectedness with nature empowers everything, including spiritual identity.

The construction of cities today ignores the flow of nature, separating us even more fully from our essential selves. What might happen if we bring nature back into our structures, using sacred geometry in architecture as it was in ancient churches, synagogues and mosques, designing our cities for energy flows? It's possible we would restore the balance and harmony missing in today's culture and become mentally, physically, and spiritually healthier for the entire planet.

The current medical model is inadequate to care for today's problems, let alone the issues that are arising in this transition. Medicine assumes the systems of the body can be treated in isolation from each other when, in reality, they're an interwoven whole. Symptoms are treated rather than root causes, and health is considered separate from the environment, food and water, social relationships, and spiritual connection.

Most importantly, medicine views death as a 'treatment failure,' ignoring the truth that every one of us will die. Birth and death are the bookends to life. When we accept death as part of life, we live more fully in the present moment, listen more deeply to our bodies, and pay better attention to our inner wisdom. We can't fully live until death is accepted, and only then can medicine treat people with genuine compassion and care.

Alternative and Conventional Medical Approaches

People are turning to alternatives, partly because there is a shortage of conventional medical providers and partly because alternatives are better at preventing illness and maintaining good health. Modern medicine is amazing at heroics; organ transplants or treatments after car accidents, for example, are best served through the interventions of conventional medicine. Alternative medicine shines in preventing illness and treating chronic conditions. Respecting the value in both approaches uses each appropriately. As the stressors in this transitional period increase, some institutions, professionals, and people will move toward greater respect of both approaches, and others will become more polarized.

Alternative energy incorporates a large spectrum of modalities including subtle energy healing. Remembering that energy forms physical templates based on frequency, energy medicine modalities seek to shift the frequency of disease back to that of our original template. In doing so, the body is in an optimal position to activate its self-healing processes.

Currently, light treatments are bridging alternative and conventional approaches. Research done in 1984, reported in *Cell Biophysics,* reports that living cells emit highly coherent photons of light called biophotons, packets of light that are biological in nature and whose presence benefits health.[8] Research continues, with the most recent meta-analysis conducted in February of 2024.[9] Red light therapy and near and far infrared therapy are used by dermatologists and physical therapists as readily as by alternative providers. In fact, light treatments may open the door to more frequency devices used in conventional medicine.

The use of frequency diagnostically in EKGs and EEGs is longstanding. Electric stimulation uses different frequencies to penetrate specific body levels for muscle relaxation, injury healing, and skin repair. Currently, the most innovative use of frequency healing in conventional medicine is with the treatment of brain cancer. The Optune system, for example, disrupts tumor growth using arrays of electrodes that transmit frequency into the brain.[10] This type of treatment is still in its infancy and will need considerable refinement, but it's encouraging to see the convergence of thought between conventional and alternatives prevailing.

However, the difference in approach to using frequency in conventional treatments and energy medicine is significant. Modern medicine uses the old model of killing what we don't like, using frequencies that disrupt tumor growth. An alternative approach might present frequencies that support the optimal health of the tissue, creating an environment in which the tumor can't grow. In addition, alternatives seek to understand the body-mind aspect of the illness in order to promote inner growth. The difference in perspective is fundamental to the success of energy medicine.

While financial losses, supply disruption, and government interference in medical decisions are part of what is collapsing the system, the most significant driving force toward creating a new and better paradigm is the experiences medical providers have that fall outside the realm of normal. One way or the other, we are being woken up. Hands-on energy medicine in integrative cancer treatment is only a start. While we don't know what the new model will be, patient-centered partnerships between doctors and patients are high on the list of essentials.

If We Behaved As if the God in All Life Mattered . . .

Our technological advancement has distanced us from our relationship with nature. We see ourselves as separate from the natural world and have lost our connection with Earth. But as the First Nation people remind us, Earth never lost her connection with us. While we consider ourselves the most advanced species on the planet, the pinnacle of evolution, we are, in fact, only the most recent. We are children in the process of growing up. As we stumble, the rest of nature supports us, helping us awaken. That is the transformation underway—humans awakening.

The French Jesuit, paleontologist, philosopher, and teacher Teilhard de Chardin said, "We are spiritual beings having a human experience," meaning that the greater part of who we are lives in the unseen part of this spectrum. What we often forget, however, is that this also means that spirituality is pervasive in everything. We don't have to travel at the speed of light squared to be part of an unseen world; we can experience that realm in the here and now. Our material reality can be as powerfully spiritual as our energetic reality. The balancing point in the transformative dance between energy (spirit) and matter is life. When we discover this, we open to hidden inner resources and find we can intentionally interact with holographic reality. We can be co-creative in the evolution of the planet.

If we take Machaelle Small Wright's advice and behave as if the god in all life matters, as if the divine exists within every living being and extend that into all of creation, all substance, all matter, inanimate and animate, everything changes. There's no longer an us and them; no war for control of resources, no destroying the rainforest—the planet's lungs—for profit. We wouldn't be polluting our streams. There wouldn't be cruelty because we would experience the truth that cruelty to one is cruelty to everyone.

If we behaved as if the divine in all life matters, we would be more connected to the higher parts of ourselves, our inner wisdom, each other, and source. The true measure of spirituality is how vulnerable we are willing to be and how much love we can carry into the challenges we face. Not whether we face challenges but how we respond to them.

The cruelty of these times instills feelings of hatred in caring and compassionate people. These feelings are a sign of how deeply we love. We need to reach even deeper, find the principles within that sustain us, and align with them to direct our thoughts and actions. Transcendent emotions such as gratitude, awe, wonder, compassion, empathy, and unconditional love lift us up. This is how we shift our frequency when faced with unspeakable pain. Then, we take the energy of that pain and direct it into positive action. We look for what is needed in our communities and help each other through.

The prime directive of every spiritual tradition is to love each other. Love is the glue that holds reality together. It is our love that keeps us committed to a higher goal. Love is the transformative frequency that makes the path very clear: remove from within every resistance to love. Unconditional love is the most powerful force in the universe.

The transition we are in, the purification of outmoded ways, has the potential to birth enlightenment. Whether enlightenment is delivered dead or alive is entirely up to us. If we remain attached to frequencies of fear and division, we will present the worst of who we are as the best we have to offer and create it. We must carefully consider what we cherish and put our energy into bringing it to life. What do we hold dear? What do we value? How do we want to show up in the times ahead? What would change if we really believed we are part of an interconnected whole, and that what happens to one happens to all? It is in these questions that we find the path forward.

Subtle Energy Healing: Meditative Exercises for Healing, Self-Care, and Inner Balance is available as a paperback, audio, CD, and eBook for Kindle at https://tinyurl.com/um3b4b4k

1. Cymatics full documentary. *Bringing Matter to Life with Sound* https://www.youtube.com/watch?v=Pmsfuj1Rk9c&t=250s
2. Emoto, Masaru. *The Message from Water,* Hado Publishing; 2nd edition (December 1, 1999)
3. https://oisf.org/understanding-the-higgs-1-frozen-light-2/
4. https://yogananda.org/blog/secret-of-vitality
5. Talbot, Michael, *The Holographic Universe,* **Generic** (January 1, 1997)
6. Stobbe, E., Sundermann, J., Ascone, L. et al. Birdsongs alleviate anxiety and paranoia in healthy participants. *Sci Rep* **12**, 16414 (2022). https://doi.org/10.1038/s41598-022-20841-0
7. Panagopoulos, D., Johansson, O. & Carlo, G. Polarization: A Key Difference between Man-made and Natural Electromagnetic Fields, in regard to Biological Activity. *Sci Rep* **5**, 14914 (2015). https://doi.org/10.1038/srep14914
8. Popp FA, Nagl W, Li KH, Scholz W, Weingärtner O, Wolf R. Biophoton emission. New evidence for coherence and DNA as source. Cell Biophys. 1984 Mar;6(1):33-52. doi: 10.1007/BF02788579. PMID: 6204761. (*https://pubmed.ncbi.nlm.nih.gov/6204761/*)
9. Mould RR, Mackenzie AM, Kalampouka I, Nunn AVW, Thomas EL, Bell JD, Botchway SW. Ultra weak photon emission-a brief review. Front Physiol. 2024 Feb 14;15:1348915. doi: 10.3389/fphys.2024.1348915. PMID: 38420619; PMCID: PMC10899412.9 (*https://pmc.ncbi.nlm.nih.gov/articles/PMC10899412/*)
10. Fabian D, Guillermo Prieto Eibl MDP, Alnahhas I, Sebastian N, Giglio P, Puduvalli V, Gonzalez J, Palmer JD. Treatment of Glioblastoma (GBM) with the Addition of Tumor-Treating Fields (TTF): A Review. Cancers (Basel). 2019 Feb 2;11(2):174. doi: 10.3390/cancers11020174. PMID: 30717372; PMCID: PMC6406491.

DR SYNTHIA ANDREWS is a licensed Naturopathic Physician and energy intuitive. She graduated in 2008 from the University of Bridgeport, College of Naturopathic Medicine in Bridgeport, Connecticut, with 30 years' prior experience as a massage therapist. She taught for fifteen years at the Connecticut Center for Massage Therapy, Connecticut's premier massage training facility and at the famed Kripalu Institute in Lenox, Massachusetts. For the past twenty years, she and her husband, Colin Andrews, have collaborated in the exploration of consciousness and non-ordinary reality.

Synthia's work focuses on the underlying spiritual and emotional aspects of health, healing, and expanding awareness. She developed and employs a unique approach called Body Sounding™ that enhances emotional and energetic awareness during the healing process.

She is the author and co-author of eight published works that offer guidance in navigating subtle energy terrain and non-ordinary reality, including The Path of Emotions and The Path of Energy, which explore emotional shifts and physical sensations involved in the process of awakening.

Synthia teaches energy awareness workshops and webinars; lectures, and maintains a private naturopathic practice in Guilford, CT.

www.thepathofenergy.com
www.andrewshealingarts.com

Gail's Conscious Living Challenge:
Break the Pattern, Choose Discernment, Choose Change

It's easy to read a book like this, nod along, and say, *yes, I know things need to change.*

But what will you actually do with this knowledge?

Will you set it aside, get caught up in daily distractions, and continue following the same patterns? Or will you choose to act, shift, and embody the change?

Here are some practical ways to create the changes you want to see:

Judgment vs. Discernment

In the documentary film *It's Time...*, we open with Synthia's powerful quote: *"The only thing that separates us is judgment."*
Good or bad, right or wrong—whether we realize it or not, we constantly judge ourselves, each other, and nearly everything in our world. Even beyond our words and thoughts, we judge through our senses—everything we see, hear, touch, smell, and feel is measured, compared, and labeled. Learning the difference between judgment and discernment has been a profound lesson for me.

What's the Difference?

Judgment is often reactive, shaped by conditioning, bias, or fear. Discernment is the capacity to judge well—i.e., to make informed and balanced choices in various situations.

Discernment allows you to see beyond appearances, recognize truth from falsehood, and make informed, conscious choices rather than reacting from programmed responses. Often, those who develop discernment have a heightened intuition, an ability to see patterns others miss, and a deeper understanding of reality.

How Can You Develop Discernment?

- **Observe Your Thoughts**: Set an intention to notice how often you judge people and things without thinking.
- **Examine Your Words**: Are you constantly putting yourself or others down? Do your words lean toward negativity or empowerment?
- **Tune into Energy**: Synthia writes about energy as the new "language of the heart"—a subtle, intuitive way we communicate beyond words. Practice feeling others' energy rather than relying only on what they say.

A friend once asked me: "What if everything we have learned is wrong and we need to unlearn everything and start over?"

The good news? If we can learn something, we are equally capable of unlearning it.

Ask Yourself:

- How am I contributing to the world I say I want?
- What energy am I putting out? Remember—the energy you project always comes back in some form. What energy would you like to receive? Practice projecting that instead.
- What words am I using daily? Are they lifting you and others up or reinforcing negativity?
- What limiting beliefs am I still holding onto?
- Where am I waiting for someone else to take action instead of leading myself?

Small Actions, Big Shifts

Transformation doesn't require massive leaps—it begins with small, intentional choices.

Want proof? Try this:

- Rate your health on a scale of 1-10—then commit to one small shift.
- Pick one unhealthy habit and swap it for a healthier one.

- Drink more water or try an alternative healing modality. Introduce a simple practice like yoga, pilates, breathwork, massage, or grounding in nature.

Then, watch how that one small change leads to a bigger transformation.

This Moment Demands More From Us

This moment in history requires us to break free from conditioned thinking, move beyond fear, and reclaim our responsibility for change.

So, what will you do?

The choice is yours.

3

Introducing Steven A. Ross Ph.D.

I FIRST MET STEVEN ROSS and his wife, Deborah, in 2019 when they visited one of the earliest Harmonic Egg® Centers in Arizona. At the time, I was there training clients on how to use the device. The moment Steven walked in, I was struck by his kind eyes and the warmth of his energy—it was the kind of presence that instantly put me at ease.

I knew nothing about him beyond the fact that he was there for a session in this "new-fangled Harmonic Egg® device that had just arrived in Arizona." But something about him felt familiar, as if our paths were meant to cross.

I helped the new owner-in-training set the sound and light selections for Steven, and he enjoyed the session immensely. However, having done so much energy work on himself over the years, his experience wasn't as earth-shattering as it is for many first-time users. I'll admit, I felt a little disappointed at first. But over time, I've learned that not everyone emerges from the Egg with a life-changing story—and that's okay. The real impact often unfolds in subtler, deeper ways.

After his session, we exchanged information and have stayed in touch ever since. Steven has been a huge supporter and mentor. Over the years, I've visited the Sedona area many times, spending hours in the wisdom library with him—immersed in conversation, reflecting on the past, speculating about the future, and simply enjoying the profound peace that comes from being surrounded by such incredible books. The sheer energy of that space is overwhelming in the best way. I have so many fond memories of those moments—just sitting, absorbing, and allowing the wisdom within those pages to sink in.

We've shared meals, engaged in deep discussions, and had countless phone conversations over the past five years. Steven is one of the few people I trust with thoughts and emotions that others might judge me for. He has an incredible ability to offer soft encouragement, gently reassuring me that I'm on the right path. We are often our own harshest critics, and Steven has a way of guiding me through my own self-judgment, reminding me of the road I know I've chosen—even when I've wandered into the weeds.

And he does it all with humor. No matter how serious the conversation, he has a way of lightening the load, bringing laughter and perspective to even the heaviest topics.

When I decided to make the film, Steven was at the top of my list to appear. My vision was to feature men and women of great wisdom—individuals with extraordinary backgrounds and credentials who, despite their achievements, remain humble, authentic, and grounded in common sense. I wanted voices that would challenge conventional thinking, ignite curiosity, and offer thought-provoking truths in a world that seems to have lost its grip on reason.

I was also intentional about including women whose work and wisdom have blown me away—women who may not have big marketing teams or massive platforms but whose messages deserve to be heard. This film is my way of giving them that space, of amplifying voices that can help shape a better world. Not everyone has the resources or visibility to share their truth on a large scale, but I believe every person featured in this film has a message the world needs right now.

Timeless Wisdom for a Modern World
by Steven A. Ross, Ph.D.

One of my greatest satisfactions in life has come from solving mysteries. Always eager to embrace an opportunity to learn, I have relished every chance to discover the hidden, untangle meanings, and understand the unexplained. One major mystery that inspired my professional activities over the last 45 years had to do with a health situation that I faced as a student at university. Reflecting on that incident, I realize it was the first of two major life currents running through, informing, and guiding my life, my beliefs, and my work.

As a youth, I was very blessed with having beyond average speed. I held all of the school records for my events at high school and at Cal State Northridge university, where I was awarded an athletic scholarship. I ran 100 meters, 200 meters, and anchored our 400-meter relay team.

One day, after competing in the Claremont relays, running the fastest time I had ever run for that point in the season, I was on such a high that I decided to do a new field work-out my coach had suggested. As I came to the 75-yard mark in full stride, I noticed there was a sprinkler head right where my left foot was going to land. Trying to avoid it, I extended my stride. Then, suddenly, I felt something POP! The pain was excruciating. My knee was burning, I felt as if I had been hit in the stomach and wanted to throw up. I let out a terrible scream but nobody was around to hear me. I tried to stand but it was impossible. I had to crawl on my hands and knees, dragging my left leg behind me, toward the trainer's room in the physical education department, which was a long way from the track. When I finally made it, the head trainer's face went white with worry. He helped me up on a table and summoned the coach. After a brief discussion, the coach decided I needed to see an orthopedic specialist. I was sent to see Dr. Kerlan (Dr. K), who was head physician for the Los Angeles Rams, the Dodgers, and the L.A. Lakers, and one of the most renowned specialists in the U.S.

The news was not good. Without surgery I would never compete again.

A second opinion was sought from the trainer at UCLA. He concurred. Deflated, I returned to my university. Sitting, dejected, in my trainer's room, I happened to notice a copy of Popular Mechanics magazine lying next to the whirlpool. Flicking idly through it, my attention was caught by an article about a therapeutic technique that was being used in Russia. When I spoke with Dr. K, later I asked if he knew about this new technique which promised recovery without surgery.

"It's holistic garbage. It's never going to work," he said dismissively.

"So what do you know about it?" I pressed. He didn't answer.

Perplexed, I said "If you don't know about it how could you say it doesn't work?"

"Son," he said, in a tone that indicated his irritation, "This is America! If we don't have it, then it isn't worth anything!"

I was just nineteen, but I knew that what he was saying was not right. I decided to try the treatment for myself.

I was fanatical. I visualized myself running, in the lead, breasting the tape and winning. And all the while I followed the articles instructions, alternating cold and thawing, alternative cold and thawing, non-stop, sometimes for sixteen hours, through the day and a good chunk of the night. I continued this for three weeks.

I missed four weeks of training and finished the year as an All-American in my sporting event. That injury not only introduced me to the world of alternative medicine but also planted a seed in me. *What other things exist in this world that we are not made aware of in the United States?* I wondered.

The second major life current involved a Native American man I met who told me that all my future guidance would come in dreams.

I was 23 years old, and I remember laughing and thinking, "I don't recall many of my dreams and those I do are sometimes silly and don't have any meaning."

But I was so excited to find my place in the universe, and so anxious, that I couldn't sleep for an entire week. After seven days, I finally had a dream. Following that dream led me to the world of spirituality and esoteric philosophy. Since then, dreams have led me around the world to places where I have found devices, materials, and ancient texts and books filled with valuable information that are now contained in a very special library of which I am privileged to be called the Guardian.

Sometimes I would have as many as six dreams a night, some of which would reveal telephone numbers, which, when called, would be answered by someone who would say, "We've been waiting for you. We want you to take care of some materials." How these people knew of me, I never discovered. But following those dreams and visions has resulted in the formation of my non-profit organization, the World Research Foundation (WRF).

The Secrets in Ancient Texts

Housing over 30,000 volumes, these libraries offer a treasure trove of knowledge spanning allopathic, complementary, and alternative medicine, preserving ancient and traditional healing techniques, from *agni hotra* (cow dung therapy) to chemotherapy, alongside the latest medical advancements. Their collections also delve into philosophical works dating back to the 16th century, holding keys to addressing today's environmental and spiritual crises. These repositories remind us that the wisdom of those who walked before us may provide more enduring solutions than modern technology and artificial intelligence.

Humanity stands at a crossroads. As a librarian and historian, I see how ancient philosophies reveal that we have been conditioned to forget our identities as unique individuals who are part of everything that exists around us. Many of today's challenges stem from significant differences in opinions and viewpoints, as well as a culture of self-centeredness perpetuated by television and social media. However, my 52 years of global research and study of these ancient texts and documents have shown me that true health and well-being lie in simplicity and the wisdom of the past.

Modern science, often regarded as the bedrock of existence and the foundation of reality, has led us to overlook our deeper senses and has trained us to think within constraints. In contrast, ancient civilizations embraced a boundless curiosity, exploring the universe without limitations of time or space. By reconnecting with this expansive mindset, we could restore the deeper senses we have been conditioned to ignore and help rediscover balance in a world that's increasingly out of harmony.

We are constantly bombarded by technology and countless distractions that pull our attention outward. This relentless exposure has fundamentally altered who we are as individuals. We're told by science how we should act to be healthier and happier, yet scientific conclusions are constantly shifting. New discoveries are made. Changes take place. And oftentimes, those new discoveries are old discoveries that somehow got discounted with the advent of science.

Science and Spirituality – Which Is the More Solid?

Recently, I came across a news article about two aerospace nuclear medical doctors in Paris, France, who used a radioactive isotope and scanning cameras to visualize the entire acupuncture meridian system. This discovery validated the ancient Chinese meridian system, which was documented over 2,500 years ago. Yet even as recently as 1970, physicians and scientists were saying that acupuncture and meridians did not exist. What fascinates me is how the ancient Chinese were able to map out the system so perfectly, and why it has taken modern science thousands of years to confirm something that those ancient practitioners understood and successfully utilized millennia ago. What does this mean? It means that science is constantly evolving. The insights of a seer—someone with deep spiritual awareness—who perceived higher, unseen energies 2,500 years ago, align with what contemporary seers observe today.

I once heard a story about two studies that arrived on the same day in the offices of the New England Medical Journal. Both studies were on the same subject, the protocols of each study appeared to be perfect, but the results were completely opposite. The Journal is reported to have said that if either one of these studies had arrived before the other, that would have been the study that got published. The other study would not. What does this show? It shows that science is the least exact of anything. And yet, when we look at the metaphysical and spiritual side, we see that the information, philosophies, and teachings, have basically been consistent for many thousands of years. Compared to science, the esoteric appears to be much more solid.

> *"It is not about learning anything new; we're here to remember what we already know."* — PLATO

Many individuals today struggle with a lack of trust, and it's understandable. We have been conditioned to believe that the only answers we can rely on come from professionals or experts outside of ourselves. As a result, we have lost faith in our ability to find answers within.

The ancient mystery schools taught the principle of "as above, so below; as below, so above." This means that everything that exists outside of us also exists within us. As a result, we do not necessarily need teachers. Plato's statement, "It is not about learning anything new; we're here to remember what we already know," aligns with his theory of recollection, also known as the theory of innate knowledge. For me, the primary reason many people feel unhappy is their lack of trust in themselves and their ability to find answers to every challenge they face in each moment.

We instinctively know what is right for us when we are in a relaxed state until others offer their opinions, insisting that "This is right and that is wrong." When we lack integrity within ourselves—meaning our actions do not align with our beliefs—we create a disconnect. Integrity signifies that our actions reflect our beliefs, and we must "walk the talk." When we act contrary to our true feelings, it creates a conflict, leading us to question our choices: "Am I doing the wrong thing?" This conflict highlights a broader issue in our society: we have lost trust in our own instincts and innate nature.

Living and working in an environment rich in knowledge and wisdom allows me to observe how we often reinvent the wheel. People frequently come up with what they believe to be modern discoveries, only to find that these ideas existed 100, 300, or even 1,000 years ago. For example, ancient Egyptians and other cultures used electric fish, such as the electric catfish and electric ray, in medical treatments to alleviate ailments like headaches, arthritis, joint pain, and epilepsy. Today, we are rediscovering that electricity and magnetism can aid in healing.

Modern society often overlooks the wisdom of previous generations, believing that our advanced technology, fast cars, and powerful computers indicate we are smarter and more inventive than those who came before us. However, many fail to recognize the difference between knowledge and wisdom. Knowledge consists of the accumulation of facts, while wisdom brings us closer to absolutes, as opposed to the relativity that we often encounter today.

Lost Opportunities and Inventions

In science, we frequently encounter discussions about limitations—statements like "This is as far as we can go." Yet, when we explore the lives of remarkable historical figures, both men and women, we discover individuals who far surpassed these so-called limitations. A prime example is Royal Raymond Rife, who, in 1933, developed a microscope ten times more powerful than the light microscopes used at that time, and even those in use today. Upon the revelation of his discovery, it was reported that "Dr. Rife has far surpassed the limitations that science claimed were unachievable."

How is it possible to exceed a "limitation," which literally means "the limit"?

Emerson once said, "When I come across narrow viewpoints, I find narrow reading." The more you immerse yourself in history, as I have, the more you realize that it may not be about "progressing" but rather about "overlooking" much of the wisdom from the past.

Emerson's timeless words resonate deeply today as medical and health costs continue to rise, with few affordable or effective solutions for growing health challenges. Pharmaceutical drugs and expensive and invasive surgeries should not be our only options. Especially when there are safer, more effective medical technologies that have been overlooked or actively suppressed within our healthcare system.

Why have organizations like Big Pharma, the FDA, and major medical institutions, whose mandates are to protect public health, chosen to exclude and even discredit proven breakthroughs such as:

- **Dr. Bjorn Nordenstrom's electrical cure**, which successfully shrank lung and breast cancer tumors without adverse effects.

- **The Diapulse machine**, shown in over 20 university studies to accelerate wound healing at twice the normal rate, only to be banned by the FDA for 15 years because it "couldn't possibly work."

- **An African herb** that eliminated the need for heart bypass surgery in 90% of scheduled cases in multiple studies.

- **Royal Rife's light-source microscope**, which could revolutionize medicine by moving away from a pharmaceutical-dominated approach.

- **A color therapy treatment** that, according to sworn testimony, healed cancer, arthritis, and diabetes, while helping a young burn victim regrow skin without topical preparations.

- Could greed, ego, and vested interests be the reason these groundbreaking technologies are kept from the public—from *you*?

In my book, *And Nothing Happened… But You Can Make It Happen*, I explore these cases and many others, exposing a system where pharmaceutical products often come with side effects ranging from memory loss and organ damage to even death. What happened to the Hippocratic Oath's principle: *"First, do no harm"*?

A New Approach to Health

In a medical industry focused on treating rather than preventing, how can we transform our health and well-being?

When people seek my counsel, their questions often revolve around achieving better health. My answer is simple: *L-E-F-L*—Laughter, Excitement, Fun, and Love. These are the pillars of true wellness.

I ask, "When was the last time you laughed?"

Many respond, "I can't remember."

"And what do you do for fun?"

"Work," they say.

"No wonder you're here," I tell them. "Work is giving you an ulcer."

What I want them to understand is that the simplicity of life—laughter, fun, beauty, and nature—is what restores balance and health.

I believe we've "civilized" ourselves out of health. Despite incredible advancements in diagnostics, many therapeutic approaches are misguided, relying on chemical interventions that force the body rather than work with it.

The human body is an electrical, magnetic organism. Life itself is measured by heartbeat and brainwaves—both electrical phenomena. Introducing foreign chemicals is like speaking a language the body doesn't understand. Instead, natural therapies—like sound, color, light, electricity, and magnetism—align with our biological systems and offer gentler, more effective paths to healing.

Let's reclaim our health by embracing simplicity and proven, natural therapies, and by questioning the systems that perpetuate illness rather than cure it.

This was the medicine of the past, and I firmly believe it will also be the medicine of the future. The ancients didn't have our modern technology or chemicals, yet people achieved health and vitality through natural tools that worked with the body rather than against it. These methods didn't force or push; instead, they allowed the body to relax and heal itself.

Our Body Is Its Own Greatest Healer

We seem to have forgotten that our body is its own greatest healer. It knows what to do when left undisturbed. As homeopathy has shown us, less is often better—not just with drugs and medical interventions but also with energy medicine. Today, we're witnessing the emergence of frequency-based healing devices that utilize magnetism, electricity, and sound to address a wide range of ailments. Yet, just as with anything we introduce to our bodies, caution and balance are essential. Sound therapy can enhance the body's natural processes, but being near a jet engine can blow your eardrums out. Magnetic beds can be effective, but if you overuse them, or the magnets are too strong, you can overwhelm the body. As with all things in life, balance is key.

We must take responsibility for our health, practice discernment, and do our own research rather than relying solely on hearsay or external authorities.

This is the guiding principle of the World Research Foundation: empowering individuals to explore, research, and trust their intuition about what feels right for their bodies. What works for one person may not work for another, even if they face the same health challenges. We are individuals—there is no one-size-fits-all approach to healing. To move forward, we must rediscover how to trust ourselves.

On ancient temple walls, three simple yet profound admonitions were inscribed:

Know thyself
Know thyself
Know thyself

Thousands of years ago, the masters understood that the answers are never external. The secret lies within us: knowing ourselves.

In the library I curate, there are texts that echo this timeless wisdom. One book, dating back to the 1400s, captures the rites, rituals, and mysteries of the ancient Mystery Schools. Their central message? We are far more powerful and magical than we realize.

The Universe Within Us

Another book, *The Anatomy of Secrets*, gifted to me by a traveling philosopher, contains a chart that unites thousands of years of teachings into a single image. This chart interweaves hermetic, alchemical, Judaic, and angelic systems with chakras, meridian lines, and the body's electrical and magnetic fields. It illustrates how our physical bodies resonate with the universe and planets, encapsulating the adage, *"As above, so below."* The world is the great universe, and each of us is a miniature universe.

Paracelsus, the pioneer of mineral- and chemical-based medicine, once said: *"Everything that exists in the outer world exists within us.* **We are the magic.** *"* The ancients believed every star outwardly has a *foci* or corresponding point—is mirrored— within us, allowing us to connect with anything in the external world. They also revered imagination as the gateway to magic. When we envision something and resonate with it, that wisdom and knowledge flow to us naturally.

Our libraries spans subjects like science, philosophy, psychology, Sufism, and alternative medicine. Among their treasures are the works of Nikola Tesla, whose groundbreaking ideas—including free energy—remain unused today, not for lack of merit but because of the disruption they might cause to established systems.

The Secret to Manifestation and Miracles

We often speak of miracles—"A miracle occurred!"—whether in healing or elsewhere. Yet the ancients knew that miracles aren't magical accidents. And the secret of all manifestation and miracles is to apply higher laws to supersede lower ones.

The highest law of all is love. Love transcends all lesser laws of this material world. It is the ultimate force, more powerful than any physical law. Love binds us, heals us, and elevates us beyond the constraints of the physical plane.

The Path Forward

As we stand on the brink of what many astrologers and seers predict will be humanity's most transformative era, the burning question is: How do we transform our health and well-being as individuals and as a collective?

In my opinion, we must go back to go forward. We must break new ground and create new traditions based on blending ancient knowledge and traditions with modern innovation, while staying rooted in timeless truths. By reclaiming the best, most natural, and enduring wisdom from the past, we can craft a new future.

A Simple Philosophy for Enlightenment

My life's journey has been devoted to this quest: traveling, searching, uncovering, learning, and preserving ancient knowledge to share with others. Along the way, people have frequently asked me, "Of all the philosophies and teachings you've encountered, what is your guiding principle?" My philosophy is simple. As you might guess, it came to me in a dream:

All one needs to achieve higher enlightenment is a beautiful heart, an open mind, and a humble spirit.

This transcends most teachings from the Masters throughout history.

A beautiful heart, an open mind, and a humble spirit

These qualities are the foundation for personal and collective transformation. Let us carry them forward into this new era of healing and awakening.

STEVEN A. ROSS, PH.D., is co-founder and CEO of the World Research Foundation, consisting of 20,000 books dating back to the 1400s. For more than 45 years he has traveled the world investigating state-of-the-art health therapies, deciphering ancient alchemical books and scrolls to help learn and share secrets of the past, and researching and lecturing in all areas of health, philosophy, spirituality, and subtle energy subjects. A world class athlete, successful businessman, academician, and total body healer, Steven has had two near-death experiences, and has held possession of one of the greatest scientific discoveries of the ages.

He has spent his adult life studying various philosophical regimes but has never joined any group or organization. He believes that we all possess a great internal guiding mechanism within us—our day and night dreams—and that we must have the trust to follow the gifts that come to us at these times.

Steven's loving philosophy can be summed up with the acronym **LEFL**. It stands for Laughter, Excitement, Fun and Love. This has been his guiding principle throughout his life. After 40 years of counseling others, he discovered that if someone's "LEFL-ometer" is charged then health is present—physical, emotional, and spiritual. However, if any one of these aspects is lacking then they begin to lose life energy which leads to health and well-being challenges.

Steven Ross's books include:

A Grand Design of Dreams: Contemplating Divine Revelation
And Nothing Happened—But You Can Make It Happen
Rife Original Frequencies and the Mysterious Nemescope
Manly P. Hall's Unpublished Pages of The Secret Teachings of All Ages,
Royal Rife Shattered

https://www.wrf.org/

Who is Colorblind?
Excerpted from "And Nothing Happened – But You Can Make it Happen"
by Steven A. Ross, Ph.D.

"There is not one blade of grass; there is no color in this world that is not intended to make us rejoice." — John Calvin

One morning during April of 1977, I awoke remembering a profound dream that I had during the night. In the dream, thousands of sick people were either sitting or lying in beds in a large multiple storied building. I heard beautiful music playing and all of the people began walking out of the building. As the people went outside, they noticed a giant rainbow in the sky even though there were no clouds. The rainbow colors began bathing all of the people, and they immediately were in perfect health.

I awoke having a belief in a new manner of healing. Sharing this concept with my father elicited the response, "Even if it is true, how will you ever figure out which color would be helpful for different health problems?"

Although my father's point was certainly logical, I did not have any doubt that somewhere I would find an answer. Actually, my quest was far easier than I would have ever imagined. When I arrived at my favorite bookstore and asked if there were any books written about the use of color and healing, I discovered there was an entire section of books dealing with color therapy.

The first book that caught my attention was Linda Clark's book, *The Ancient Art of Color Therapy*. This book proved to be a wealth of information, especially reading that color therapy was an ancient healing practice.

Linda Clark's book provided information on several medical doctors and health professionals who had been using color therapy with their patients. The manner in which the color is used seemed both simplistic and amazingly simple. Starting with Clark's book and trusting that my dream was inspiring me to look further, I began researching the possible use of color in the healing process.

Whenever I begin researching a new potential health therapy, my first concern is whether the therapy works and if it is safe. My initial research is not based on some expert's opinion regarding the therapy but on someone who has been utilizing the therapy or technique. There is an important distinction here. Often I find, similar to my experience in college with the sports physician whom I consulted for my injury, people will make comments about something that they themselves have never experienced.

My good friend Professor Dr. Karl Walter once told me that he had met many a fellow university professor in Germany who made the statement, "must not work because it cannot work." His point was that even when confronted with some fact, many people disregard their own senses because their minds think something is impossible. Karl met scientists and physicists who would see something taking place right before their eyes, but they would deny that it was happening because it contradicted their own beliefs. Perhaps this seems a confusion of words, but it is very true for some people in academia. This is the dilemma of the sacred cow. If experts accept a new fact that contradicts a point of their very own theory, then their credibility comes into question. Therefore, they make comments about something they might never have examined on their own.

When I am giving lectures and I refer to color, often a medical doctor in the audience will ask if the use of color is real and could it possibly be beneficial. Often the question is made in a very sarcastic manner. I will pose the following question to the medical doctor: "What is the therapy for babies born prematurely with infant liver syndrome? I might add, doctor, what would you use for the condition called Crigler Najjar Syndrome (CNS) (yellow jaundice)?" The doctor will respond: We use a blue." Then his voice tails off. I then say: "That is right, you use a blue light or the baby with this condition will die! Doctor, I do not know what you call that, but I would call it color therapy."

In the late 1950s, a nurse in Great Britain first discovered the value of sunlight in alleviating jaundice in newborn babies. The story has circulated that the babies near the windows lived while the babies inside the rooms would die. Subsequent study showed that it was not the total light but the blue component in the sunlight. Blue light phototherapy (another word for color therapy) is the therapy of choice to keep babies alive in their beginning stages of life. In the early 1970s when CNS was first reported, most of the babies died in infancy.

The blue light contacts the blood vessels and tissue close to the skin, and the bilirubin undergoes a number of changes. The sequence that takes place under the blue light is slightly different than the normal way that the body functions when bilirubin is present. This color therapy is the only thing that helps prevent the CNS patient from sustaining brain damage.

Now is a good time to explain color therapy. Color therapy is the use of the colors of the visible spectrum. Think of the various colors that you see in a rainbow or through a prism. Each color is determined by a rate of vibration. As vibrations change the color you see also changes. In color therapy, a color is projected over a distance onto bare skin at particular parts of the body. The location on the body is determined by what the particular health difficulty might entail. There are specific colors or combinations of hues used for specific ailments or health problems. The color affects the body in a manner that allows the body's own healing abilities to become more effective. It is not that a specific color is curing a specific health problem; the color is causing physiological change within the body that allows the body to be operating in a more efficient manner.

During the course of the last fifteen years, several popular magazines and even a few television programs have noted the effect of various colors on our moods. An article actually appeared in *Reader's Digest* many years ago relating how the color of the walls where children studied could affect their IQ. Reports have shown that when a violent prisoner is placed in a jail cell with pink walls in a matter of minutes the prisoner becomes very docile. In fact, when a poster board painted pink is placed at eye level in front of a weightlifter, the weightlifter's strength becomes greatly diminished.

I had discovered that the color blue was saving the life of sick babies, that the color pink could rob a weightlifter of his strength. Linda Clark's book had mentioned that doctors could cure cataracts with color, so I wondered what other medical conditions could be helped. I found the answer to my question when I learned of the work of Dinshah Ghadiali and his color therapy system called Spectro-Chrome.

Dinshah

My first contact with Ghadiali came when I found a sequence of photographs taken in 1926 of a little girl with 3rd degree burns over 2/3rds of her body. As you will see, the following pictures are so dramatic, and the case was so compelling, that it is impossible to ignore. The pictures were taken out of the book, *Let There Be Light*, by Darius Dinshah.

Dinshah Ghadiali

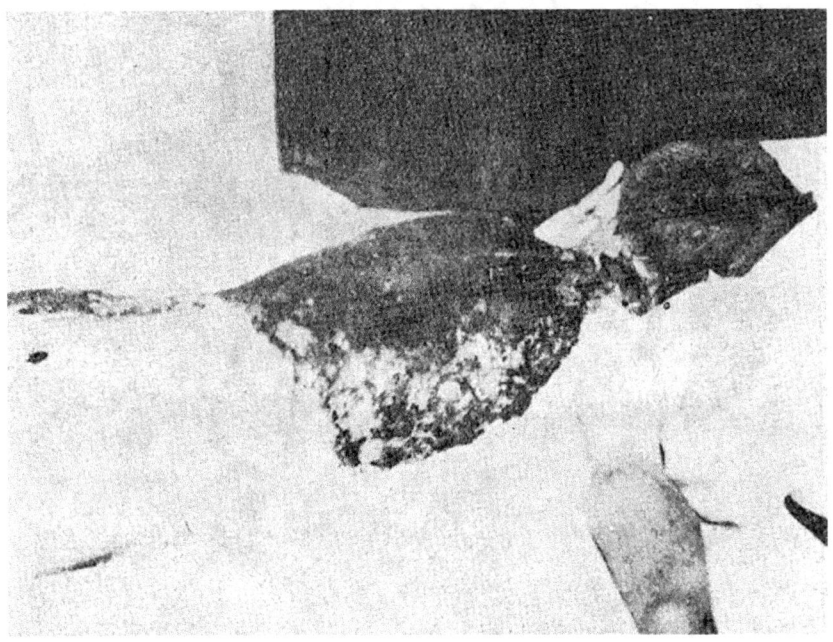

Grace Shirlow 2 weeks after admission.

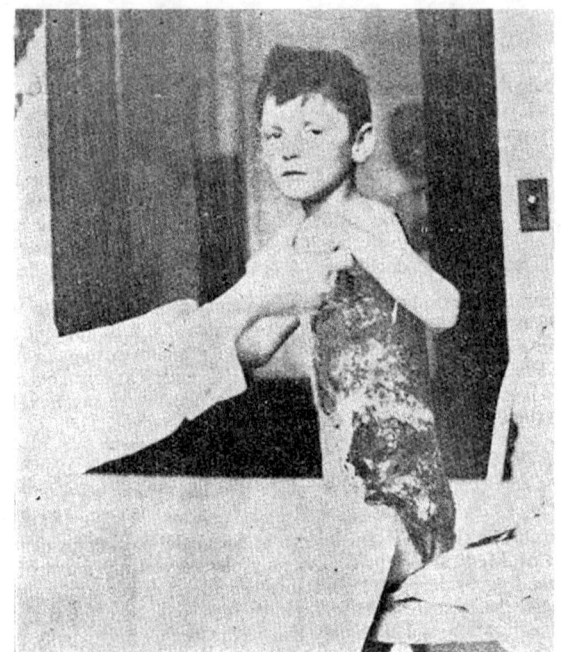

Grace Shirlow 2 weeks after admission.

Grace Shirlow 3 months after admission.

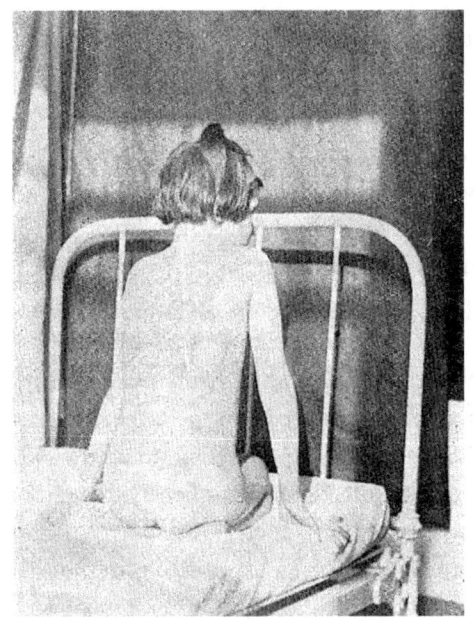

Grace Shirlow 18 months after fire.

The little girl in the pictures is Grace Shirlow. In 1926, she arrived at Philadelphia Women's Hospital where the majority of the staff of the hospital considered her a hopeless case. Eight-year-old Grace had been burned badly on much of her body; she had a body temperature of between 105 to 106 degrees and had almost complete suppression of urine for more than 48 hours.

Fluids were forced into her, but with no effect. Only one medical doctor on the staff had the belief that she could help this poor child. Dr. Kate Baldwin, who was the Senior Surgeon at the hospital, was not on call when the girl arrived but reported to the hospital several hours later. When she examined the girl and everyone present had given up hope, Dr. Baldwin proposed the use of color therapy. For several years before this case, Dr. Baldwin had been using a color therapy system called Spectro-Chrome, a method of color therapy using 12 specific colors.

Dr. Baldwin used the color scarlet over the girl's kidney, and within minutes, the little girl voided more than 6 ounces of fluids. Dr. Baldwin then projected the color blue over Grace's body and within one hour her incredible pain had subsided. In fact for the duration of Grace's stay in the hospital she did not experience any more pain from her burns. For me this is unbelievable! Think about the pain and suffering that all burn victims experience. How can anybody justify not looking into this approach?

The medical report of this case stated that no topical application was made, and no skin grafts were performed. Grace Shirlow grew new skin during the course of her Spectro-Chrome color therapy. Although this is a very dramatic burn case, it is not unique. A full report of the Grace Shirlow case was delivered at a medical meeting[1] and written up in a medical journal.[2]

The inventor of the Spectro-Chrome system is Dinshah Ghadiali. Dinshah was born in 1873, and he entered high school in 1884. This is not a typo; he entered high school at the age of *eleven*. Dinshah took his entry examinations for Bombay University at the age of thirteen. Dinshah made his first visit to the United States in 1896 and had the opportunity to meet Thomas Edison and Nikola Tesla, two of the most famous inventors and scientists in the history of our planet. Dinshah gave lectures on x-rays and radioactivity and the *New York Times* termed him the "Parsee Edison".

Dinshah and his wife and family immigrated to the United States in 1911, and Dinshah became a naturalized citizen in 1917. In 1919, Dinshah was appointed Governor of the New York City Police Aviation School and later was commissioned Colonel and Commander of the New York Police Reserve Air Service. Two aircraft obtained from the U.S. Government were used to patrol the harbor in the city of New York. Dinshah flew the first police airmail service from New York to Philadelphia. For his meritorious service to the city, New York Mayor John Hyland awarded Dinshah the Liberty Medal.

Dinshah delivered his first lecture on his Spectro-Chrome system in April of 1920. Dinshah would eventually present more than one hundred lectures throughout the United States.

At one time nearly 500 United States medical doctors were using his Spectro-Chrome system. Although the medical doctors, like Dr. Kate Baldwin, were achieving results that were remarkable, Dinshah Ghadiali was brought to trial in Camden, New Jersey, in 1931, for a charge of grand larceny. The complaint from the medical authorities was that Dinshah was committing fraud because Spectro-Chrome could not have any effect on diseases.

During his trial in 1931, Dinshah called upon three witnesses. The first witness was Dr. Kate Baldwin. Dr. Baldwin testified under oath that she had been a medical physician for 40 years and senior surgeon of Philadelphia Women's Hospital for 23 years. Under cross examination by prosecutors Dr. Baldwin stated that she had successfully used the Spectro-Chrome system for cataracts, glaucoma, hemorrhage in the retina, ordinary inflammatory conditions of the eyes, sclera, infection of the sinuses, bronchitis, pneumonia, pleurisy, tuberculosis, ulcers of the stomach, asthma, jaundice, kidney conditions, appendicitis, gonorrhea, syphilis, breast tumors and severe third-degree burns. Dr. Baldwin said that she was using up to ten Spectro-Chrome light machines in her medical practice.

Dr. Martha Peebles appeared as a second witness for Dinshah. Dr. Peebles was a Doctor of Medicine for more than twenty-four years and had worked for the Department of Health in New York City for over twenty years. Dr. Peebles was a physician to the American Expeditionary Forces during World War I. During the war, she would perform up to 61 different surgeries a day.

Dr. Peebles was forced to retire from active practice due to ill health, but when another doctor had used the Spectro-Chrome system on her, it restored her to health. At the time of the trial, Dr. Peebles was using 17 Spectro-Chrome machines in her practice. Dr. Peebles swore that she had treated cancer, arthritis, poliomyelitis, mastoiditis and many other medical conditions.

Dr. Welcome Manor, M.D., was the third doctor who appeared as a witness for Dinshah. Dr. Manor had practiced medicine for more than thirty years and testified that he had successfully treated cancer, diabetes, gonorrhea, syphilis, ulcers, hemorrhage, neuritis, spinal meningitis, heart disorders and numerous other maladies.

The jury in this 1931 case was out only 90 minutes and returned a verdict of not guilty for Dinshah. However, Dinshah's legal woes were not over. He was brought to trial for one charge after another and served a combined 18 months in jail.

In 1947, the FDA instituted a trial against Dinshah for practicing medicine without a license. Dinshah lost the case, and this effectively forced him to surrender all of his research equipment and books. According to the judge's decree, all of Dinshah's books were destroyed and Dinshah was placed under probation for five years and not allowed to discuss the Spectro-Chrome form of therapy. I've seen photographs of agents burning his books. It is heartbreaking.

In 1958, the FDA obtained a permanent injunction against Dinshah preventing any machines or books from crossing state lines. Dinshah passed away in 1966.

In 1924, in the section titled "Minutes of the Journal of the American Medical Association," an article appeared that completely discredited Dinshah as being silly and suggested that if his therapy really worked why was he wearing glasses. The article pointed out that any doctors following this system would be scrutinized for following such a stupid therapeutic approach to medicine.

Dr. Kate Baldwin was confronted by other personnel at her hospital and the Board of Directors gave her this following choice: "Either give up your use of the Spectro-Chrome machines or leave the hospital and your prestigious position." Dr. Baldwin stated that she would give up the practice of medicine rather than stop using a therapy system that was better than any other system available to a medical doctor. She resigned her position at the oldest surgical hospital in the United States.

During the years, there have been several hundred studies and reports regarding the use of color in the healing arts. In 1981, at the School of Nursing, College of Human Services, San Diego State, California, Sharon McDonald, Ph.D., conducted an interesting study of the effects of visible light waves on arthritis pain. In her controlled study she worked with 60 female volunteers between the ages of 40 and 60 years old who had confirmed medical diagnoses of rheumatoid arthritis. Dr. McDonald constructed a box that would allow her volunteers to place their elbows inside, and then she would project either a red light, blue light or no light upon their elbows. The volunteers did not know which, if any, color was used. Dr. McDonald discovered that the longer the blue light was used the greater reduction in pain. When no color was used, there was no influence in reduction or increase in the pain felt by the volunteers.

I have delivered several lectures as well as articles dealing with the use of color therapy. In a medical magazine dealing with cancer research for clinicians, an article appeared listing my organization as pushing the ridiculous concept that color could work for health problems. The article, which appeared without an author, stated that no reputable medical doctor or scientist would ever believe that color could be effective as a therapy. I wrote a letter to the journal and never received a response. I pointed out in my letter that an entire volume from the Annals of the New York Academy of Sciences was dedicated to "The Medical and Biological Effects of Light."[3]

The use of color therapy does seem to be very simplistic for the major medical problems that we are confronted with today. The reason it seems so simplistic is the conditioning we receive from medical doctors saying that difficult medical problems require difficult medical solutions.

As I was proofing this chapter, in the background I heard a television commercial promoting products for arthritis pain. It was an advertisement warning users of several of the pharmaceuticals for arthritis pain that this class of pharmaceutical products can cause internal bleeding and ulcers that can lead to death. Death! The advertiser made the point that viewers should ask their doctors if the risks are worth the benefits for their conditions. This is ludicrous! These medical therapies are worse than the original problem. How has our medical approach fallen to the point where we have to make health choices between one ailment and another as side effects of our therapies? We have gotten lost, and we must find our way back to more natural approaches that exist. There are answers to our problems, but we must search in a more open-minded manner.

The use of color dates to 500 BC, and there has never been a report of anyone who has died from using color therapy. Today there are more than 900 books written on the use of color therapy. Thousands of studies and experiments have been conducted. Most of the research is relegated to animal studies showing how color and light affect various functions in rats. I once contacted a researcher who had been doing studies on rats for his whole career, and I mentioned that color had been used on people in the 1920s and 1930s and was extremely effective, safe and well-documented. His answer was that this was what he was allowed to do, and he would not take a chance in jeopardizing his position to expand his research to humans.

I believe that the reason color therapy is not in more common use is that it is not a good moneymaker for the medical profession. A person can use simple color gels or slides and use any type of light source or even a slide projector. The cost of the correct color slides is less than $30. A color therapy session lasts about one hour and uses simple electricity to drive the light source, and because anyone can use color therapy at home, no revenue is produced for a medical doctor or clinic.

I have personally witnessed the effectiveness of color therapy in nearly five hundred people since 1977. I have seen color therapy work as effectively on animals as it does for people. In fact, because of a family emergency I had a personal experience with the effectiveness of color therapy. In 1984, my father was admitted to a leading hospital in Southern California to get an examination for back spasms. While he was in the hospital, he was given a myelogram, a dye injected by a needle, and apparently as a result of something on the needle, he ended up with an infection. Within hours of the test, every part of his body was shutting down, and he was rushed into surgery. The medical team spent four hours in surgery, but after a few days, the head of neurosurgery stated that my father was going to be a quadriplegic. The surgeon told my mother that the hospital would begin quadriplegic training when my father was able to handle it.

My father remained in intensive care for more than 3 ½ weeks, and the doctors added that my father's speech would be permanently impaired. After my father left intensive care, I spoke with the head of neurosurgery and told him we would be using color therapy on my father. The doctor asked if our therapy would disrupt any of their devices or mechanical or electrical machines in the hospital. I assured the doctor that our therapy was safe, quiet and effective. He did not have anything that would work for my father, but I believed that the color would work. What a strange situation when I thought back to my father wondering if I would ever discover the right color for various health conditions. I did have the right color for my father's condition.

My mother projected the color on my father for one hour in the morning and one hour in the evening. Interested hospital staff would walk by watching us without ever commenting about what we were doing. After a few days, my father began wiggling his toes. After another few days, my father could move his feet. One day the head surgeon, who hadn't seen my father for a week, was making his rounds and mentioned to my father he would like to see him try to wiggle his toes. The surgeon placed his face very close to my father's feet. My father told him he should step back or he might get kicked in the face. The surgeon laughed and thought my father was joking. When my father raised one foot completely off the bed the surgeon was in a state of shock.

My father eventually progressed to a wheelchair, then a walker, then crutches and finally was walking with two canes. Six weeks later, aided by two canes, my father walked out of the hospital.

If you recall in the early 1980s, the medical doctors made it difficult for you to see or get your own medical records. One of the hospital staff had made a copy of my father's medical chart, and I accidentally walked off with it. It states, "The patient has made a complete recovery from quadriplegia to 4/5 strength throughout his body…the family has refused further urological workups. He has a neurogenic bladder that will require a catheter."

Once my father returned home we used a special device called a multiple wave oscillator, and in two treatment sessions, my father was able to urinate on his own without a catheter. So much for the expert diagnosis of my father's medical condition!

I am very passionate about the use of color therapy, and I am sad about the treatment given to those people who have tried to make it available. Dinshah was a brilliant man who made an important discovery. To receive a compliment acknowledging him as being of the importance of Thomas Edison is high praise indeed. He was not a quack or someone looking to make fast money selling some sort of product. He was a serious researcher who spent his life in the service of people. Credentials, as we learned from our section about Dr. Nordenstrom, do not seem to be enough to allow someone to have a fair evaluation.

Can you imagine how difficult it would have been for Dr. Kate Baldwin in the 1930s to arrive at the position of Senior Surgeon at one of the oldest surgical hospitals in the United States? She felt so strongly about the use of color that she gave up her position rather than not be allowed to use her machines.

Pure greed keeps color therapy from being a part of our medical system. Even though I had the personal experience with my father, I cannot help but visualize the pictures of Grace Shirlow. What would Grace's life have been like without the use of color therapy?

Who is colorblind? Dinshah Ghadiali and many other color practitioners presented us with a natural and effective therapy—and nothing happened. Some benefits of using color therapy: It is completely safe with no side effects.

- It is an inexpensive therapy that is easy to administer.
- It does not pollute the environment or have toxic ingredients.
- It can be utilized for many medical conditions.
- Color slides do not wear out or need to be replaced.

1. Dr. Kate Baldwin, Section on Eye, Ear. Nose, Throat Diseases of the Medical Society of the State of Pennsylvania, Oct. 12, 1926.
2. Dr. Kate Baldwin, Atlantic Medical Journal, April 1927.
3. *The Medical and Biological Effects of Light*, Annals of the New York Academy of Sciences, Vol. 453, 1985.

Only you can make it happen!

Gail's Conscious Living Challenge:
Don't Outsource Your Health

There's so much wisdom in what Steven shares—simple truths that hit deep. I've always been a bit of a health detective, both for myself and others. After 23 years of relentless migraines and no clear answers from doctors, I finally stopped outsourcing my health and started investigating for myself.

Turns out, it wasn't just one thing. It could've been food sensitivities, stress, nervous system imbalances, viral loads, parasites, dehydration, Epstein-Barr virus, heavy metals, even tight hamstrings! I experimented, I researched, I listened to my body—and eventually, the migraines stopped. That didn't happen overnight, and neither did the causes. Healing takes time, patience, and personal responsibility. There is no one-size-fits-all when it comes to finding solutions to health concerns. We must take our health into our own hands. It's like troubleshooting an electrical problem. You learn how it works and go one by one on what could be wrong until you find the root cause.

I love how Steven says *true health lies in simplicity*! When I created the Harmonic Egg®, I wanted to get back to basics. No Wi-Fi, no Bluetooth, no computer system. Just sound, light, vibration, and space to reconnect. We've overcomplicated healing—piling on tech, gadgets, and "bio hacks" without asking what our bodies truly need. And frankly, I don't believe hacking the body is a long-term path to real wellness.

Here's your challenge:

Be your own investigator. If you've got a health issue, instead of jumping to a quick fix, take a breath and ask: *What's really going on here?* Follow the trail, gently and curiously.

Be discerning. Look beyond flashy headlines and miracle cures. Who's funding the research? Who profits from your belief in that pill, device, or protocol? Use your head *and* your gut.

Take time for silence. Even just five minutes a day. That's when your nervous system can reset. That's when you hear your own knowing. That's where healing begins.

Pay attention to energy. The energy of a practitioner, a food, a product—it all affects you. Tune in and ask: *Is this raising or draining my energy?*

Remember: your body knows. You just have to start listening again. We are more capable than we've been led to believe. That's not just a nice idea—it's a fact.

Gail's Reflections on the Chapter on Color Therapy

I share Steven's passion for color therapy. When I created the Harmonic Egg, I was deeply inspired by a line I read in a book on *Auras* attributed to Edgar Cayce. It suggested that when the spiritual forces of sound and light are brought together, they could form a powerful modality for healing. That vision stayed with me. And now, here we are—sound and light therapy—these gentle, non-invasive approaches are becoming more widely available. And for good reason: they support the body's natural healing process without the harsh side effects.

That's one of the reasons I feel so strongly about questioning what we accept as normal. Watching pharmaceutical ads with cheerful people dancing through fields while a voiceover lists frightening side effects—it's become so normalized, we barely question it. But we should. I encourage everyone to pause and ask: *Who benefits from this? Who tested it?* And most importantly, *Does this feel right for me?*

I think about pioneers like Dinshah, who faced criticism and resistance for their work. When someone once questioned why he wore glasses if his therapy worked, I couldn't help but wonder if there were emotional reasons beneath the surface—grief, disillusionment, or simply the stress of constant opposition. Sometimes our bodies express what our hearts carry. The root of illness isn't always physical.

Steven mentions Thomas Edison's many attempts before the lightbulb succeeded—how he reframed failure as simply discovering what *didn't* work. That mindset resonates with me. People like Dinshah and Edison didn't give up, and that inspires me to keep going too—even when things get hard or criticism surfaces. I've seen too many people benefit from the Harmonic Egg to walk away from what I know is helping.

Healing is a journey. It takes courage, experimentation, and trust in your inner knowing. That's what I hear in Steven's words—and it's what I try to live every day.

4

Introducing Ani Williams

I FIRST DISCOVERED ANI WILLIAMS around 2013 or 2014 while watching an interview with her on Gaia TV with Regina Meredith. She spoke about "missing tones" in the voice and how these can be linked to physical or emotional imbalances in the body. I was instantly intrigued. At the time, I was on a mission to uncover the root cause of the migraines that had plagued me since I was 17.

I booked a voice analysis session with Ani, which proved uncannily accurate and revealing. It made me wonder how I could integrate her music into my sound and light therapy practice.

In 2019, I attended her in-person class in Sedona, Arizona—and it was a complete game-changer. I'd stayed in touch with Ani over the years, following her evolution as a soul, and telling anyone who would listen about her work—because most people still haven't heard of this, and they *need* to.

When we began casting for *It's Time*, I knew I had to include Ani in the film. It felt like a long shot—she had been living in France and hadn't been to the U.S. in five years. But when I called and asked if, by any chance, she would be in the States in March 2024, she replied, "Yes." I asked where, and she said, "Arizona." As it turned out, she would be in *the same town* we were filming. Magic. There are no accidents.

I've always loved Ani's energy and her passion for what she does. I feel like we've been soul friends for a long time. She was just as excited to be part of the film and told me her mother would've been thrilled to see her shining in all her brilliance.

It's truly an honor to call Ani a friend—and even more of an honor to witness her continued growth, wisdom, and light.

Since Ani is in the middle of writing the sequel to her book *Guardians of the Dragon Path*, our editor, Sandie Sedgbeer, interviewed her for a chapter on sound therapy based on Ani's experience, research, and guidance.

Rewriting Our Story, Recreating Our World

An interview with Ani Williams
by Sandie Sedgbeer

The great Sufi Master Hazrat Inayat Khan stated, "The person who has found the keynote in their voice has found the key to life." As we stand on the brink of one of the most transformative eras that humanity is likely to encounter, I would take that statement one stage further by adding, "The individual who has discovered the keynote in their voice possesses the power to reshape their own story and redefine our world."

That person could be you.

Sound is a powerful tool for effecting change and is fast becoming a leading-edge modality for healing and exploring our greater soul potential.

Long before we developed the tools for reading and writing, we had our voices, which the ancients were adept at using to regulate their lives. The Egyptians and most indigenous cultures possessed knowledge that allowed them to arrange their rituals around the cycles of nature. They had specific songs and dances designed to create and maintain harmony and dialogue between the celestial and terrestrial realms. In Egypt's temple of Dendera, depictions of musical instruments—such as harps, drums, and flutes are carved in stone alongside Hathor, the goddess of music and beauty. The same temple features the zodiac portrayed on its ceiling, and one wall displays a hieroglyph that translates to: "The sky and its stars make music in you."

Until the 1700s, astrology was an essential part of medicine, which, along with astronomy, was taught in the medical academies in Europe. In fact, the astronomer Galileo, who invented the telescope, was one of the instructors. This was important in medicine because the aspects and configurations created by the frequencies of the sun, moon, and other planets at our time of birth significantly influence us. For example, if we look at the positions of the planets when we were born, note the constellations they were in and the corresponding frequencies of those positions, and then map the sound patterns, the resulting pattern would mirror our unique voice tones.

For millennia, visionaries, scientists, philosophers, and those seeking to understand the patterns of creation have extensively studied the movements of the cosmos and their reflection in cycles and nature's patterns on Earth. Ancient cultures such as the Chinese, Egyptian, Sumerian, Druid, and Mayan civilizations, along with influential figures like Plato, Pythagoras, Copernicus, and Kepler, recognized the interconnectedness of planetary cycles, sacred geometry, and musical scales long before modern science began to confirm these connections. The divine order of the cosmos and the sacred proportions in ancient temple design embody the same principles as music, the Harmonia Mundi.

Plato believed that music was the most powerful influence in life. His treatise, the Timaeus, describes the numerical (hence, vibrational-musical) creation of the physical universe and the soul that animates it. He encouraged his students to activate the ancient shrines and sacred temples of the earth with sacred music, using 'perpetual choirs' to echo the harmonies of the Heavenly Choir.

Sadly, a fragmentation of integrative traditions over the years has led us to lose many valuable practices. However, with new discoveries and technologies revealing the interrelationship of frequencies in various forms—such as sound, light, and color—we are beginning to understand the potential of reintegrating these ancient techniques and knowledge. Today, scientists and physicians are continuing the legacy of these ancient traditions, the wisdom keys for changing our reality and creating a harmonious environment in our lives and on Earth.

Ani Williams is an internationally renowned harpist, singer, musician, author, and sound therapist who has performed worldwide since the 1980s and has recorded more than 24 albums of original music based on ancient, sacred traditions. Her seminal work in the study of ancient cultures, sound, and the relationship between music, tones, the human voice, and healing led to the important discovery that our voice holds the key to healing ourselves and the world around us.

I'll repeat that so you understand the importance of what you are about to learn in this chapter.

Your voice is your key to releasing all the limiting beliefs and patterns you may have accumulated throughout your life, including any trauma that you may have experienced. Your voice is the barometer of your soul and the reflection of your body, mind, and spirit. Your personal stories, coded in your energy fields, can be heard in your voice, which is constantly broadcasting information out into the world and reflecting your state of being. Your voice communicates your physical, emotional, and spiritual states to the world—whether you feel anxious, depressed, afraid, hopeful, joyous, or empowered. Your voice also reflects your state of health, how well your organs function, what minerals your body might be missing, etc. The tonality of your voice influences how others perceive you. Indeed, new research shows that what you are feeling is reflected in the sound of your voice and is transmitted far more than the words you might be saying.

For instance, when we cultivate feelings of compassion, love, and appreciation, our voice changes, and our heart radiates a powerful electrical energy. This affects our body-mind-spirit and the world around us, creating a state of harmony and coherence. Research has found that when we are in a state of loving kindness, the frequencies and energy from our hearts radiate much more powerfully than our minds. Having positive, harmonious intentions for the world and maintaining a balanced, loving heart energy can influence your surroundings. This shift can help reduce chaos, divisiveness, and polarization, fostering a more harmonious environment.

Each of your senses—sight, hearing, taste, smell, touch, etc., are controlled by your brain. Finding your powerful signature sound, the keynote in your voice, and using this tone by simply humming can change your reality. Adding a positive intention to your sound supports the release of physical or emotional stress and tension, thus liberating your creativity and enabling you to remember who you are and your original intention. Likewise, tuning your brain to harmonious music and practicing toning will also expand your bandwidth of perception, your clarity, and your ability to see and hear beyond the narrow frequencies currently experienced and start changing your reality

The Power of Sound

The great master of China, Lao Tzu, allegedly said that the whole universe can hear the music of our soul. And it's not just those around us who are affected by the sounds we are putting out, but also the whole of nature. Being much more attuned to their environment, ancient peoples were attuned to the movements of the heavens. They could likely sense the movement of terrestrial currents and the energetic effects of the presence of certain elements, such as iron, gold, silver, and copper. Each element has a frequency, just as each planet and star has a song.

The interrelationship between our intentions, sound, and their effects in visible patterns was made clear in the work of Japanese researcher Masaru Emoto (1943-2014). He discovered that water exposed to positive words and intentions formed beautiful, symmetrical crystalline structures when frozen. In contrast, water subjected to negative words and intentions developed chaotic, asymmetrical structures. He concluded that since water covers the largest portion of our planet and constitutes a significant percentage of our physical bodies, our thoughts and feelings significantly impact our environments globally and personally. His work also included conducting global "appreciation meditations" aimed at purifying some of Earth's major rivers that have been polluted.

Dr. Emoto's research is an example of what Swiss researcher Hans Jenny (1904-1972) discovered while projecting pure tones onto fine grains of matter or liquid and observing the forming of distinct geometric shapes. Jenny termed this sound-matter connection Cymatics, and his groundbreaking work has become a cornerstone of sound healing.

In the 1970s, the French musician, composer, researcher, healer, and martial artist Fabien Maman conducted pioneering research that found that the cell would dissolve when they sounded a series of specific tuning fork tones onto a cancer cell. This interrelationship of sound and matter is at the core of an exciting revival of ancient sound science based on timeless principles well known to all ancient and indigenous cultures.

Today, allopathic medicine is beginning to embrace the principle of non-invasive sound treatment methods. For example, Scientific American magazine reported on an effective technique for removing kidney stones that involves identifying the frequency of the stone and projecting the 'reversed' frequency to dissolve it. In 2019, the Wall Street Journal published an article entitled "What Your Voice Reveals About You," including examples of the medical and corporate communities incorporating voice diagnostics.

Discovering the Missing Tones

Voice spectrum analysis, also called voice diagnostics, is a powerful tool that provides insights into human behavior and psychology. This technique analyzes the voice's pitch, tone, and rhythm to help us understand the physical, mental, and emotional states of being. Versatile and non-invasive, it's attractive for researchers investigating its benefits for emotion recognition, health monitoring, lie detection, speaker identification, and much more. Corporations use sophisticated voice analysis technology to analyze the patterns of prospective employees and uncover the qualities inherent in applicants, enabling HR staff to determine whether someone is appropriate for a specific job or might be more effective in another position. Call centers are using it to help staff understand the emotional state of a prospective caller or customer. Medical researchers are studying the frequency patterns in patients that reveal their state of being and can even predict disease before it manifests.

Ani Williams learned voice analysis in 1992 from Sharry Edwards of Sound Health Options, a pioneer in this science, long before corporations caught on to what we can learn about a person just by diagnosing their voice patterns. In the same way that a hearing test maps the levels of one's hearing, a voice analysis session analyzes the pattern of frequencies in the voice to assess where the tones are strong, stressed, or missing. Since every traumatic experience, accident, or significant emotional occurrence has a frequency, missing tones and notes can be identified and "treated" by applying the same tones to release the stressful issue, strengthen the system, and integrate the tonality.

For example, if a person was missing half of the spectrum of tones—which is quite common, Williams would compare the missing voice tones with their chronic issues and family's genetic tendencies. If a genetic deficiency of magnesium was found, which can create a tendency for depression or bone loss, she would apply the frequency related to magnesium and suggest a diet rich in magnesium. She describes this as "like a form of sonic homeopathy, in which, for instance, one might treat toxic food reactions with the remedy Arsenicum, which contains a minute amount of arsenic."

The type of sound used is critical because many applications today are synthetically created computer-generated tones, like sine waves in a particular frequency. After trying various electronic sounds, Williams realized that the applied tones needed to incorporate acoustic instruments, in which the tones create a perfect harmonic signature which is pure and powerful. More importantly, the human voice is the most potent and the only living instrument. Incorporating these principles, she created a series of twelve recordings for each of the tones in the Western musical scale, using overtone chanting, harp, didgeridoo, and Tibetan bowls. (Songaia Sound Medicine.) She found that working with natural harmonic frequencies of ancient instruments with a long history of use in healing and the human voice is the most effective. Williams has also found that the frequency of our emotions holds the key that will set us free.

Oded Mansura is a brilliant practitioner of Medical Astrology and Sound Therapy from Israel who was one of the first to teach with Sharry Edwards in the early 1990s. Edwards had discovered a correlation between a person's voice patterning and astrological sun signs. Mansura took the work of voice analysis a step further by incorporating the ancient science of medical astrology when he found that the tone patterns from voice analysis matched or mirrored an individual's astrological tones.

We've all heard the term "Music of the Spheres," but few understand its true meaning. The correspondence between the cosmic emanations and the human energy system is tangible and can be measured! With voice diagnostics, we can hear the corresponding celestial tones in the voice and work with these sounds for healing. For instance, the tone ascribed to the sign of Aquarius is A#, which relates to the nervous system and electrical fields. A# is 55 Hertz (cycles per second), the same frequency as electricity. I don't think it's any coincidence that with so many electrical fields in our environment, many people today suffer from an overstressed nervous system as that same frequency of the Age of Aquarius—A#, also relates to minerals, particularly the trace minerals, and silica, which support the nerves.

Goethe, the famous German mystic, philosopher, and poet gave us another way of looking at celestial sound patterning as it comes into the terrestrial realm when he said that sacred architecture, which frequently includes celestial alignments, is "frozen music." Most of the ancient architecture that was built using sacred proportions mirrored the cosmic patterns. Many of the proportions of architecture in the temples in Cambodia, the sun and moon pyramids at Teotihuacan, and the Egyptian pyramids are based on 72 degrees. The number 72 relates to the human heartbeat and the cycles of time and is also very important in astrology. Every 72 years, the precession of the observed fixed stars drifts one degree. So, here again, we have the mirroring of the celestial patterns on the Earth.

All Creation Stories Begin With a Sound or a Song

The Biblical verse in the Gospel of John that states: "In the beginning was the Word," suggests that God "spoke" the universe into creation. But it's more than a word; it is Logos, Creative Voice. In the ancient Vedic texts, seed syllables, called 'Bija' (considered an entire paradigm in form), are seeds of creation that are strung together and used in ancient mantras. These sound formulas can change not only matter but also energy and space. Sound plus Intention is the ancient alchemical formula for creation. And Sound plus Intention=Healing.

In indigenous cultures, the sound of creation in their stories is always a song. In the first centuries A.D., the Druids and early Christians practiced "perpetual choirs," in which they constantly chanted harmony into their realm to sustain the natural order. The same tradition was practiced eons ago in China, Egypt, and beyond. In today's world, the Tibetans still maintain that practice of perpetual chanting. Plato believed that creating conscious societies that used harmonious musical modes could be totally sustainable.

The cosmology of the Australian aboriginal people is arranged around songs, or Songlines, which correspond to the landscape and reflect how the contours of hills and valleys rise and fall. Their songs form patterns and rhythms that correspond with the land and important places. To connect with the essence of a place, you must sing its song, and there is a totally harmonious union or "entrainment" between the sound of the place and the ancestor representing the place—the shape of the land and the shape of the song. When an aboriginal woman wanted to attract a husband, she would learn his song and then sing that song with intention. That's ancient song magic. Aboriginal women say we know nothing about how to survive in our environment without song knowledge.

Indigenous peoples in the American northwest and the South Pacific would navigate their canoes by singing songs. So, seven rounds of a particular song or chant might mark the time it would take to get from one place to another. They would also use their sensory connections with the elements to assist them, like watching the stars or feeling the water temperature change.

Within cultures like the Yaqui of northern Mexico and southern Arizona, it is said that "song is the intelligent language of the universe"— how we connect with all of creation. The Yaquis used song to connect daily with all aspects of nature and ensure a harmonious world. The Hopi practice this as well. In the summertime, they sing and dance the rituals to bring the rain to nourish the land and the crops.

As modern technology advanced, much of the world lost its indigenous sound traditions, and the genocide of indigenous cultures destroyed a wealth of knowledge on healing. One story Williams tells is of a great Zulu medicine man called Credo Mutwa who, when people came to him for healing, would not ask when their symptoms first occurred, but instead, would ask them when it was that they stopped singing! It's a good question to ask ourselves: when did we stop singing?

Your Astrological Birth Chart Patterns Are Reflected In Your Voice Patterns

According to Ani Williams, we all have a unique symphony singing and emanating from us that informs matter and energy. This underpins her Songaia Sound therapy system, which works with the specific frequency patterns unique to each individual. Songaia Sound, which means sound or song of the earth, was created 33 years ago to include Voice Analysis sessions, Sound Alchemy trainings, the therapeutic Songaia tones, and Ani's extensive music recordings. Her system helps people of all ages and walks of life find the key tone that relates to their most significant area of wounding and healing, hence the sound key for liberating their greatest potential.

Williams found that the celestial pattern occurring when a person is born mirrors the frequencies in their voice. Her system analyzes the frequency patterns formed by the planets, sun, and moon at the moment of a person's birth and the frequencies occurring in their voice. For example, if Saturn in a client's birth chart was exactly squared to Pluto, she would look at the tones related to those planetary positions and compare them with their voice pattern to determine the most potent frequencies to work with. Invariably, the planetary stress tones mirror the missing tones in the voice, giving a clear picture of that individual's 'Sound Signature.' The client then applies these tones for healing, integration, and well-being in body, mind, and spirit. In this system, each of the 12 signs of the zodiac is assigned a frequency from the 12-tone chromatic musical scale.

Williams observed that the human voice reveals our story and provides an overview of our emotional, mental, and physical state. When people are not expressing their full potential, certain tones are stressed or dropping out of their speaking voice. Additionally, a lack of tonal depth and resonance can indicate a disconnection with one's personal power or groundedness, including the ability to manifest one's deepest wishes and dreams.

When individuals are not grounded and connected with their physicality, they may speak in a higher register or exhibit a thin quality in their voice, and Williams found this to be the case with victims of sexual abuse. To address this, the missing tones related to stress issues are recommended as a "sound prescription." Each of the twelve Songaia Sound tones is a 15-minute sound meditation designed for individuals to tone along in their missing voice frequencies. This can activate the missing frequency corresponding to their trauma, wounds, or limiting beliefs, ultimately facilitating their release. This process can transform an individual's physical, emotional, and mental life, promoting healing and overall well-being.

For example, let's say you are missing the tone of C. Some of the physical issues related to this tone can include systemic conditions such as candida, chronic fatigue, cancer, AIDS, and problems with the blood and large muscles such as the heart. On another level, you might feel ungrounded, disconnected from your true purpose, or not fully in your power. You might also find it difficult to manifest your creative gifts or realize your goals. In this case, bringing in the C tone could help you feel more powerful, grounded, whole, and in control of your life. It works on an energy level first, but ultimately, it also affects the physical. Sometimes, there is an instantaneous change in the physical, with a reduction of pain and stress. Heart rate, pulse rate, and oxygenation rates can change instantly. Headaches may disappear, and physical pain and discomfort can melt into the sound.

One case history that Williams shares clearly illustrates the astrological-voice pattern connection. The client was missing the tone F# in his voice, which relates to the Sun sign of Libra and can correlate with physical issues with the kidneys, bladder, or immune system. This person was born in October in the sign of Libra, had just undergone kidney cancer treatment, and was in remission. Her recommendation was for him to tone his missing F# daily to prevent a recurrence of the disease.

While most of Williams' clients use their tones to liberate their life potential and assist in releasing emotional patterns, she has also found that using the sounds regularly can address medical issues. Using their missing tones has enabled clients to raise their thyroid levels and even reduce the size of brain tumors. The sounds also supported healing behavioral problems in youth and neural-muscular issues in infants. She states that by using sound consciously and regularly, we continually recreate our state of being.

This is borne out by research conducted several years ago by Williams with the late Juan Acosta, PhD., at the University of Washington Department of Medicine. They found that the brain state totally altered and went into deep Theta within a minute of toning or chanting a mantra, which approximates deep meditation. Even thinking about toning brought about this state. During another project with Dr. Acosta, Williams reported that while using advanced body scanning cameras on various subjects, the images revealed dark red colors in the body and the energy field, where there was congestion or inflammation. After toning or just holding feelings of love and appreciation for a few moments, the images showed the aura and physical body filled with increased light. Where there was an imbalance or darkness, there now was a brightness in the body and the energy field, which supports well-being on all levels.

Japanese monks teach that when we chant daily, we develop more harmonics and resonance in our voice so that every time we use our voice, we are healed, others are healed, and all our communicative interactions come from a place of more harmony, centeredness, and empowerment. Developing our voices allows us to be 'heard' and helps manifest what we are here on earth to accomplish. Toning and singing synchronize your brain rhythms with your heart rhythms, which ultimately increases immune function. Science has found that simply humming produces nitric oxygen, which helps reduce blood pressure and inflammation and speed up wound healing. So, whether it's humming, chanting, singing, or repeating mantras, a daily toning practice is essential for your health. It's an ancient practice for healing, clarity and awakening.

How Sound Can Elevate and Heal Humanity

If we want to change our story and create a new paradigm, reconnecting with our authentic selves and with one another is the first step. One powerful and easy way to accomplish this is to use sound to transform ourselves and our world.

In a world dominated by technology and increasing levels of stress, there's a growing need for harmonious sound. This is reflected in the rising popularity of relaxation music and sound therapy. Although the type of music we need is different for each of us depending on our culture, conditioning, orientation and mood state, generally speaking, if our brainwaves are in beta or fight-or-flight mode, our body is releasing cortisone, which creates more stress and a ready-for-action state of being. In this case, music with deep bass and strong rhythms will stimulate the centers between the solar plexus and the base chakra, keeping the body in a ready-to-roll state.

What we need in the world right now is music that will refine our energy centers and allow them to open—music that opens the heart so that we can change the state of our world. But a lot of today's recordings don't use real acoustic instruments anymore. People don't realize there can be a degenerative aspect to digital music, which is arranged mathematically without a natural harmonic structure. When we pluck a string, we produce natural overtones that ring out and, if you want to consider the mathematical principle of harmonics, essentially go on forever.

As mentioned above, there many varieties of digital, synthesized frequencies, available on the sound therapy circuit, but Williams prefers to use natural harmonic sounds, such as overtone chanting, the Australian didgeridoo, which has been used in sound therapy for perhaps 40,000 years, and the harp, which has been used in therapeutic settings for thousands of years, going back much earlier than Pythagoras and the Asclepian temples, to Egypt and Sumeria.

After decades of using this technique with thousands of people around the world, Williams has seen incredible transformation in children with autism as they begin to communicate and come out of isolation. One beautiful example she relates occurred when working with one of her first autistic clients, a hyperactive five-year-old boy.

> "When we met, it was clear that his parents were very stressed out. Although the child's speech was unintelligible, I was able to get a voice analysis. After this, I sat down at the harp and just started playing, matching the music to his activity and then gradually slowing it down. He had never seen a harp before, but after a few minutes, he came over and began to play a perfect duet with me. Afterward, he kissed me on the cheek and said, "Harp." His parents were in tears, and they got him an instrument, and he naturally began playing his "missing tones." Before long, his hyperactive state had calmed, and he was thriving and communicating intelligently."

Using harmonious music, especially our voice, is one of the most potent things we can do to heal ourselves. The Vedic texts in the Mahabharata state that sacred sound is one of the most direct paths to enlightenment. Ancient cultures integrated music and singing into their rituals and daily lives, but over time there was a loss of unified social systems. In today's fragmented and often chaotic world, music is often placed in a category for "professionals" only, for recordings and performances.

Unfortunately, early in life, many begin to shut down the authentic expression of their voice. Too often, we've been told we mustn't cry, or laugh, or be too noisy. "Sit down. Shut up. Don't speak unless invited" is a common refrain in schools throughout the world. "You're singing off-key; you're making too much noise." "Don't express your emotional feelings." On and on it goes. It is no wonder so many young people lack confidence in social situations when so many forms of authentic vocal expression are frowned upon. However, Williams found that the connection between sound, voice, and emotion is one of the keys to healing. Just the simple act of sighing can reconnect the neural pathways between the brain, the emotion, the body, and the voice. There's actually a term for it: "sentics," the sound of emotion.

Back in the late 1960s, as we were beginning to learn more about the brain, Manfred Clynes, an Austrian-born scientist, inventor, and musician, made groundbreaking discoveries in the brain's link to emotional expression. He embarked on a series of experiments involving the fundamental expressive forms of the central nervous system, which he referred to as "sentic forms." Through these experiments, he sought to demonstrate the universality of these forms by extracting sounds from people's emotional expressions. These sounds were then played to individuals from different cultures, who accurately identified the specific emotions conveyed.

Based on these findings, Clynes developed an application in which subjects used touch to express a sequence of emotions—neutrality, anger, hate, grief, love, sexual desire, joy, and reverence—through finger pressure. The 25-minute sequences, called sentic cycles were based on a precise mathematical formula and resulted in subjects reporting calmness, energy, an alleviation of depression, and even a loosening of the grip of tobacco and alcohol addictions. Clynes used his research to prove that it was possible to counter a negative emotional state by inducing a rather rapid shift into a positive one, particularly showing that music was a powerful mechanism for inducing love, joy, and reverence.

In 1976, Clynes published the book *Sentics: The Touch of the Emotions*, in which he outlined his findings of emotional perception and response at the intersection of music, art, and mathematics. Clynes' work and book laid the foundation of the sentics field, insights from which have influenced everything from psychotherapy to addiction rehabilitation to education.[1]

We are in a fascinating era of rediscovering sound science and its numerous applications. However, with many new remedies on the market, it's essential to be discerning and to research any claims made. For instance, some people suggest that specific frequencies, such as 528 Hz or 432 Hz, or the Schumann resonance, can heal all ailments. The problem is that there is no one-size-fits-all solution; one frequency will not heal everyone in the same way. Each person has their own unique symphony of sound. Therefore, it is important to study the individual, understand their unique frequencies, and identify the correct combination of sounds for their healing and liberation.

Using Your Voice To Heal Yourself and Create a New Earth

The science of sound is the science of life. It's integral to life itself. We are beginning to acknowledge the power of sound, to bring unity, to re-create our reality, and to use non-invasive forms of sound in medicine. As the Asclepian healing traditions were doing thousands of years ago, we can treat the whole person, the soul, and imagine the transformation of humanity and our world.

So how can we apply this information to be useful at this time? As the indigenous cultures of the planet have done, we can live close to nature's elements and rhythms. We can become aware and align ourselves to the turning of the seasons and the movements of the heavens. We can use music and sound for healing. Harmonious sound not only benefits us but also radiates into the environment around us, releasing stress, anxiety, altering brain states, and creating a coherent field that is much needed in a time of chaos. This also helps clear the energies within the collective consciousness that are holding fear and survival-based emotions.

As Ani Williams so beautifully reminds us:

> "Our voice is the only living instrument on the planet. If we can begin to use our voices in an authentic way, connecting our feelings and emotions with the sound, one voice at a time, one complete symphony at a time, singing in harmony—our personal healing can begin. Imagine a new Song of the Earth emerging from our joined authentic voices, singing, without it being a performance, just singing

naturally to express our love, we would have the perfect choir to start transforming the world around us. And the healing of humanity and our planet can truly begin."

1. https://en.wikipedia.org/wiki/Manfred_Clynes

ANI WILLIAMS is a harpist, singer, author, and sound therapist. She has performed worldwide since the 1980s and has recorded more than 24 albums of original music based on ancient, sacred traditions. She has done seminal research in sound healing and the relationship between musical tones, the human voice and healing. In 1992 she founded Songaia Sound, incorporating the history of sound science, Voice Diagnostics, and the Songaia therapeutic recordings for clients world-wide. Her Sound Alchemy—Bio-Acoustic training course is now online.

For more than three decades Ani has presented concerts, seminars, trainings, and healing seminars in the US, Mexico, Holland, France, Poland, the Czech Republic, and England, and maintains a private sound counseling practice. In 1994, Ani developed Songaia Sound Medicine, a system of using specific musical frequencies as a therapy, and the Songaia CD's, a series of sound meditations used as an effective healing tool for her clients.

Her new book, *Guardians of the Dragon Path* is the first volume in her upcoming "Guardians" trilogy, which chronicles a stunning journey in ancient sound and healing traditions across the Pyrenees and the Camino de Compostela.

www.aniwilliams.com

Gail's Conscious Living Challenge:
Tune In to the Music of Your Soul

Ani's chapter is close to my heart. I've seen the incredible transformations that can occur when using sound and tones to support physical or emotional healing. Some of the results have been nothing short of amazing.

Ancient knowledge is returning—not as a trend, but because it worked. We suppressed it for so long, but the wisdom is rising again. Ani's work incorporates astrology and the natal chart, which resonates deeply with me. Recently, I had a conversation with my friend Dr. Jerry Wintrob, an eye doctor who just published an article titled "Using Natal Charts to Predict Visual Deficits and Anomalies."[1] We're coming full circle—returning to the understanding that everything is connected.

Ani shares that until the 1700s, the zodiac was an integral part of medicine. Now, we're rediscovering how music can help the body regain balance—not just through specific frequencies like 528 Hz, but through waveforms, intention, and presence.

Music created with love, purpose, and a healing intention was often far more powerful than much of what we hear today. Unlike commercial music produced purely for profit, it carried a deeper resonance. Thankfully, we're now witnessing a resurgence of *conscious music*—crafted by artists whose work flows from high heart energy and deep spiritual alignment.

When it comes to voice analysis, discernment is everything. The tools and practitioners matter. People like Ani Williams and Elaine Thompson have truly mastered the art. They don't just identify missing tones—they help clients understand why those tones may be missing and how to restore them.

There's a proper way to do this kind of work. It's not just counting backward from 10 to 0 and recording your voice. Ani's method is emotional, intentional, and deeply intuitive. I've had missing tones in the past—but since I began working with the Harmonic Egg®, those tones have returned. One fascinating moment came when a voice analysis showed that my partner had strong tones in areas where I was low. It made me wonder if we subconsciously seek out people whose "frequencies" balance our own?

So here's my challenge to you:

- **Think differently.** Consider how your time of birth, your place of birth, and your natal chart might shape who you are today. Everything is connected.
- **Create community.** Gather friends together. Share your birth charts or your favorite healing music. Listen together. Reflect on how your body feels and what it stirs in you. Does it bring up a memory, an emotion, a realization?
- **Be discerning.** That theme flows throughout this entire book and film. So many claims are being made these days about scalar waves, bioresonance, and healing tools. However, very few are supported by science or measurable tools.
The word "bioresonance" comes from the Greek bios (life) and Latin resonare (to echo). By that definition, I believe the Harmonic Egg® is an actual bioresonance chamber—a literal life echo. Life begins in the egg, and sound reflects within it.
- **Don't die with your music still in you.** (Thank you, Wayne Dyer.) Whatever your soul came here to express—let it out.

1. *https://opaastrology.org/magazine/OPA-TEA-2025-March-Equinox.pdf*

5

Introducing Sarah Cotterill

I FIRST MET SARAH in 2023 when I was invited to speak to members of the "Journey of Intrinsic Health," Dr. Zach Bush's community forum. She was the moderator for my talk, and we connected instantly. Sarah and I share a common thread: we love to give, we love to see people thrive, and, yes, sometimes we give too much. We've both been taken advantage of more times than we can count, but we keep showing up with open hearts. We refuse to believe that kindness doesn't make a difference, even when it's not reciprocated. It does.

Sarah's path in life has been anything but ordinary. You can learn more about her journey in her bio, but let's just say she was ahead of her time. Years ago, she stepped away from a career she was once deeply passionate about, burned out by a system resistant to change. Now, at a time when change is no longer optional, she is stepping back in—not just as a participant, but as a powerful influencer and changemaker in the very field that once wore her down.

Sarah is fiercely driven, deeply compassionate, and determined to help transform the medical field from the inside out. In the film *It's Time*, you will see us walking across a bridge over icy water in Michigan—deep in conversation, completely energized by our shared passion, despite the biting cold that made it hard to feel our extremities. That moment perfectly captured who we are: two women deeply committed to truth, healing, and helping others awaken, striving to make the world a better place— no matter the conditions.

Moving From the Love of Power to the Power of Love

by Sarah Cotterill

It was spring 2018, my favorite time of the year. Newly birthed tulips were gaily popping out of the ground as if summoned to a party by the sun. It was the season of renewal, and for the first time in my adult life, their radiant palette of vibrant reds and oranges, soft pinks, and purples left me completely untouched. The sun was shining, but my body was cold. The breeze was gentle but devoid of promise. At some point over the winter months, the unthinkable had happened. I had been brought to my knees in a way I had never dreamed possible.

Call it a dismantling or the dark night of the soul. Regardless, the plan I had for a perfect life was crumbling. I had survived (and honestly thrived) after the end of my marriage several years before. But this was different. This time, it was my career that was unraveling, along with all the personal stories and collective agreements I held to be true.

I was a healthcare attorney and executive, working with physicians and hospital systems on everything from recruitment, contracts, training, and development to employee wellbeing and with medical teams to ascertain the root cause of problems when things went wrong. I was moving up the corporate ladder, gaining responsibility and prestige. Everything was going to plan. I should have been happy. And yet, I had this nagging sensation that something wasn't right. The medical industry was changing, getting more stressful, more calculating, and less patient-focused. I couldn't help but notice that the general discontent was growing; what we were providing was becoming less like healthcare and more like a poor attempt at disease management.

Gone were the days when our organization was agile and nimble, when a patient could call and speak directly to a nurse with both the authority and the understanding that the patient needed not another prescription or scan but an air conditioning unit in their apartment. Gone, too, were the days when patients could spend time talking to a doctor who knew them and their family, understood their history and circumstances, and saw and listened to them as a whole human being rather than a list of lab results and ailments.

A nasty ugliness was creeping into the systems, training us to be compliant, complacent, and less sure of who we are and what we know. I knew my colleagues were good people, trying their hardest to do the right things. But a culture of "big Pharma knows it all," "time is money," and increasing reliance on technology, telehealth, and AI was slowly erasing the less visible but no less crucial components of primary importance to their patients' wellbeing—human connection, being seen, being heard, feeling that someone values you enough to spend time with you and that you matter.

I was seeing more and more physicians who loved their jobs and were wholly dedicated to patient care losing sight of the need to care for themselves. Long shifts, short breaks, lack of sleep, stress-driven unhealthy food grabs, the frustration of having to see more patients in less time, and the inevitable loss of connection and communication caused by an increasing reliance on telemedicine was taking its toll. Many were stressed out, sick, and frustrated with the care they were able to give their patients. Some were overweight, unhealthy, and struggling with their own mental and physical ailments.

Everything I loved about my job was diminishing as the health care service transformed into a wealth care business. Worse yet, the more energy and attention we invested in technology to broaden our connections and make our lives and jobs easier, the more disconnected I began to feel. And I wasn't alone. I saw it in the interactions between doctors, nurses, and patients. Weighed down by an overload of information, technology, social media, and contradictory opinions, and squeezed by the necessity to do more in less time, we were forgetting how to connect with that intrinsic knowing inside of us. Forgetting how to connect with others and the ancient truth that we are all healthier, happier, and more fulfilled when we are part of a community. Most importantly, we seem to forget that our bodies and the natural world are our most advanced technologies.

It didn't feel right, and my body knew it. I was having a massive crisis of faith, questioning everything I had worked so hard for. Instead of improving healthcare, statistics showed an accelerating decline in the population's health, with life expectancy falling for the first time in history. Reports showing that millennials now have higher rates of health conditions than their predecessors at the same age with their health peaking at age 27 before declining, and a relentless rise in obesity, heart disease, cancer, autoimmune diseases, and metabolic dysfunction were worrying. The news that despite spending more on healthcare than any country, the U.S. health care system ranks last among industrialized nations was especially concerning. America was paying more but getting less? How was that even possible?

Where did we go wrong?

One overarching problem is that we have chosen to pay for activity rather than results. Another is that price doesn't dictate quality. The same procedure at your neighborhood hospital could cost more and yield worse results than your friend's identical procedure at another local hospital. This wasn't the way things were supposed to go.

Medical knowledge is exploding. In 1950, it doubled every 50 years. Today, it's estimated to double every 73 days. This rapid advancement presents a double-edged sword—while it opens the door to better patient care through cutting-edge treatments and diagnostics, it also presents physicians with the daunting challenge of staying current on the latest innovative procedures, approaches, technologies, and drugs.

Currently, we are toggling our way between a system in which the sickest patients are seen by a physician for 15-20 minutes every three months, and a system in which a patient is sent home with a touch screen monitor for temperature, blood pressure, pulse, oxygen, glucose, weight, and EKG, plus a stethoscope for their heart and lungs. Then, their next appointment with their physician will be a tele-heath session, after which everything will be monitored and evaluated by artificial intelligence (AI), which will recommend treatment changes for the physician's approval. While this has some undeniable advantages, it is missing a crucial component that is less visible but of primary importance to a patient's wellbeing—human connection, being seen, being heard, feeling that someone values you enough to spend time with you and that you matter.

In Western medicine, we make everything a fight. We fight disease, we fight bacteria, and we fight cancer. We've developed a reductionist perspective—we break things into parts. We create graphs and capture statistics—and if we don't find what we're looking for, we assume that the absence of evidence is evidence of absence. But it's not!

It was so disheartening. This wasn't the way things were supposed to go. The systems I was taught to trust in, that we were assured would take care of us and our families, were collapsing. And with the dismantling of my worldview came a collapse in meaning.

As my inner voice grew louder, I found myself facing some tough questions.

"Who could I actually trust?"

"Why is no one teaching medical students the importance of food, sunlight, and hydration?"

"Why was I told that my daughter was fine when she was suffering from a severe overgrowth of candida?"

"Why is it so hard to talk with a human when I have a question?"

"What do I really want and need in life?"

Suddenly, doctors, teachers, and leaders were all being called into question. To further complicate matters for me, I felt overwhelmed by the exponential amount of everything. A total overload of information, technology, social media, and opinions. A full blast firehose of different perspectives and polarizing topics that were creating such an oscillation that I could hardly connect with even one of them.

It was time to start using my discernment. I wanted a better framework than that for my pre-teen children.

With some help from the universe, I was forced to remember what truly mattered.

So, I ended a toxic relationship and my time at the Fortune 6 healthcare company. And I started to reconnect.

Searching for Solutions

After leaving my career as an attorney in healthcare all my friends and family weighed in on what I should do next. Teach yoga. Take another legal job. Their suggestions were endless. Grateful that they cared, I nonetheless listened to my inner voice, directing me to take my time, use my discernment, and follow my heart. So, I did. I walked. I practiced yoga. I traveled. And I dived deeply into research on a variety of topics. I spoke and engaged with people from all walks of life with different jobs, interests, and perspectives. As the great healers of ancient traditions modeled, I began to identify imbalances, rethink, purify, and stand in awe. I learned that there is no balance, only balancing. And since life isn't static, we must embrace change, meet it, flow with it, and recalibrate for the season ahead. It took time, but

I didn't waver. I had to reconnect with myself, with nature, and with others. And unlike the medical system model of fighting with everything, I began to flow with life again.

Throughout this prolonged period of soul-searching, questioning, and learning, I was supported by the research I was uncovering. That gave me solace and motivated me to avoid taking the victim route. I learned to trust my intuition; there was something essential to be learned from my longing for something more, and my "avoid doing anything that feels heavy" instinct was a necessary step along a guiding path.

Trauma and hardship come to all of us. It's inevitable. And each of us has the capacity to understand and heal ourselves, whether it's a health issue, a relationship falling apart, not knowing what we want to be/do at the midpoint in life, a sick child or parent, or a financial crisis—and all the things in between—there has to be a code or an operating system we can learn, I felt certain. So, I set about answering the question of how we can get to know our bodies as well as we know our cell phones or computers?

After much research and contemplation, I came to realize that one of the biggest problems for our healthcare system isn't necessarily spending. It's not the quality of our doctors. It's not their intention. It boils down to that one thing—reconnection. We need to reconnect to ourselves and to others. We need to understand and embrace the simple truth that we can't do ME well without WE.

We must consider the whole living system, discover how one part influences all the other parts, and learn how to bring them all into balance. In the Eastern system and other ancient traditions, it's not about fighting but creating balance through purification. Great healers of these ancient traditions are adept at identifying imbalances and prescribing remedies to cleanse and rebalance the system. To flow with, not fight against.

Scientists say that we are in the midst of the sixth great extinction. We have destroyed the biodiversity on the planet by polluting, overfishing, and the like. The rate of extinction is increasing, while our human ability to reproduce is dramatically decreasing. We have lost the art of gathering. People are desperate for community. Everybody wants to be part of something. Inter-connectedness, community, collaboration, compassion, and happiness play a vital role in the quality of our lives, health, and wellbeing. Stress is the number one killer, and happiness is a key factor in combatting the effects of stress. But how many of us can honestly say we are happy?

One of the world's most extended research projects is a Harvard study conducted over the past 80 years, tracking several generations of men to determine what leads to a long and happy life. It found that the number one variable isn't diet or exercise. It's not work. Nor achievements or money. It's who cares about you and who you care about. The quality of your life is determined by the quality of your relationship. Or said differently, the quality of your relationships determines the quality of your life. But how do we define quality in our relationships?

Research study psychologist Sonja Lyubomirsky suggests that only 50 percent of our happiness is determined by immutable factors like our genes or temperaments, our "set point." The other half is determined by a combination of circumstances over which we have a great deal of agency. Three key factors that seem to have a significant influence on increasing our happiness are:

1. Our ability to reframe our situation more positively
2. Our capacity to express gratitude, and
3. Our choice to be kind and generous.

In the Dalai Lama's book *The Art of Happiness*, co-written with psychiatrist Howard Cutler, Cutler summarized that happy people are more loving and forgiving than unhappy people. This is borne out by the research of Dr. Stephen G. Post, the lead author of the best-selling book *When Good Things Happen to Good People: How to Live a Longer, Healthier, Happier Life by the Simple Act of Giving*, which shares that kindness, caring, compassion, and giving of ourselves and helping others in meaningful ways—especially if we start young—has a significant impact on everything from life satisfaction to self-realization and physical health. Depression is reduced. Wellbeing and good fortune are increased, and mortality is delayed. And we are happier, healthier, more resilient, creative, hopeful, and more successful.

In *The Awakened Brain*, Dr. Lisa Miller points to research in neuroscience, psychology, and anthropology that we are biologically equipped as spiritual beings, and that engaging in spiritual activities—like spending time in nature, meditation, and connecting to others—enhances mental health and wellbeing. Life and lab reveal the same things: that we are bonded in a network of love that holds us in a loving embrace and that we amplify human potential through the power of community and vice versa.

Amazing, right? Until you read the 2018 survey that showed half of Americans feel alone, isolated, or left out. According to The Cigna CMO, being lonely has the same impact on mortality as smoking twelve cigarettes a day, making it even more dangerous than obesity.

The Dali Lama suggests that one is never lonely when thinking about others with kindness and compassion. Openheartedness, warmheartedness, is the antidote to loneliness. And in my experience, to no surprise—he's got a point.

As I reflected on the circumstances that had brought me to that "dark night of my soul," I realized that while I had so many of the traditional wellness tools, I had to evaluate—did I have the strong relationships I needed to go the distance in life? To live wholly and fully? Loving my children taught me that we're all worthy of love. Love is our birthright. It's how we are built to live. And my ultimate journey of self-love, of creating health and healing for myself lay in coming back to who I am.

When What You're Doing Isn't Working, Change What You're Doing

A wise person once said that when what we are doing is not working, we must change what we are doing. So, how can we start changing things?

One of our first priorities is to understand that we cannot separate our bodies from our mind and spirit. We must acknowledge and start treating our mind/body/spirit as one wholistic unit.

Another is to start cultivating reconnection. Reconnection to ourselves, to others, and to our stories. We must regain control of the stories we're telling because they are shaping the future we're creating. To do that, we need to remember our deepest inspiration, heal our pain and apathy, and connect to each other like never before.

When I exited the healthcare system and started to delve really deep, I realized that we have the innate and intrinsic ability to heal ourselves if we can reconnect and look at our health in a different way.

The future of health isn't about more complexity—it's about remembering what we've always known: our bodies know how to heal, and sometimes the most straightforward practices yield the most profound results. If we genuinely want healing and the creation of health in our own lives, we must step into our power, each one of us, and together. Transforming health happens when we step into our own authority, and shift our thinking from outsourcing our health, feeling a victim, powerless, and lost to loving ourselves and each other.

We can quit paying for activity and start paying for results instead. The same market forces that drive so much activity would then be unleashed to move us from last to first in health. We can change our mindset from survival of the fittest to survival of those that fit together and acknowledge that our "togetherness," our community, and our belonging are foundational parts of healing.

There are entire industries devoted to personal growth, biohacking, and self-help. Most of them distract from the broader human project. Our bodies are the highest form of technology. Can we learn to operate them as well as we do our devices? Can we regulate ourselves so that we can relate to others? We can. We merely need to remember that what we allow into our minds matters. It matters that we create the time to feed and nurture our spirit—take walks in nature, enjoy the simple things in life, take time out to take time in, quiet moments when we can meditate, ruminate, contemplate, clear our minds of the daily onslaught of information and connect with our intuition, feelings and emotions, and find our truths. It matters that we carve our moments of peace, free from stress and distraction to reconnect to ourselves and to nature, the land, and each other. And it especially matters what we put into and on our bodies. While organic is a step in the right direction, we lack minerals and hydration if it isn't grown in nutrient-dense soil.

We can empower ourselves and others to take an active role in our health, be co-creators in optimizing our overall wellbeing, get to know ourselves, figure out what fits and doesn't, and become our best health advocate.

Transforming health also happens in groups. This is where lasting, exponential change occurs—when we are empowered to participate, try new things, find our voice, develop relationships, solve our own problems, and are encouraged to go on. We don't transform illness into health in isolation; we do so in a tribe. We amplify human potential through the power of community and vice versa. We need to move from survival of the fittest to survival of those that fit together. And acknowledge that our "togetherness," our community, and our belonging are foundational parts of healing.

I transitioned into healing and the creation of health. I co-founded an innovative regenerative wellness company with a focus on building, supporting, and amplifying regenerative systems in the farming, food, and health sectors. While the context of my work has changed, the calling is the same: to amplify human potential and help people realize their goals and dreams. I am passionate about creating health and happiness everywhere and at every level of our lives. Now, whenever I feel I might be getting overwhelmed by all the options, I do the obvious: I sleep deeply, move freely, eat real food, hydrate, play, breathe fully, make love, give thanks, and commune. Nothing heavy (or expensive). It rebalances, regenerates me, and brings me back into my own knowing.

Can We Change the Healthcare System? Can We Change Ourselves?

Can we change the health care system? Maybe. Can we change ourselves? Definitely.

To do so, we must reconnect to ourselves, others, our stories, and the ancient truths. We must regain control of the stories we're telling because they are shaping the future we are creating. And to do that, we must remember our inspiration, heal our pain, and connect like never before.

We can create a new path to rebalance and rebuild our health and well-being from the inside out. It will require patience, vulnerability, self-care, and a commitment to us and to one another. We can start by introducing people who want to improve their health to each other.

There is a Tibetan saying: "Wherever you have friends, that's your country, and wherever you receive love, that's your home." Relationships are hard. Belonging may be even harder. Yet, the quantum leap in our evolution happens when we truly participate in the community. This is where all the real potential lies, in the liminal spaces in between. Together and individually, we can tap into excellence again, locate our power, and pivot our lives in empowering ways, we can give ourselves the proof and permission to reconnect to our bodies, hearts, and communities.

Simple. Not always easy. But definitely worth it.

The journey of life is moving from our love of power to the power of love. When we start to see the beauty in each other, we begin to feel the love for each other.

SARAH COTTERILL is a visionary leader, systems thinker, and attorney who bridges the worlds of corporate healthcare, personal development, and regenerative wellbeing. Her professional journey began as an attorney specializing in corporate and health care regulatory law, serving as healthcare attorney at a prominent law firm, managing hospital acquisitions at a national hospital system, and as Executive VP and General Counsel at a large healthcare network—where she oversaw HR, compliance, strategic projects, and physician recruitment before leading the organization through its sale to and integration with a national healthcare company.

A dynamic leader fueled by an unwavering commitment to amplifying human potential and cultivating positive societal change, Cotterill has a track record of founding and leading innovative companies and projects across diverse industries, including health and wellness, legal, and agricultural/hemp. Today, she leads FLIP, a consulting/coaching business focused on personal and professional development and workplace culture, which includes her "Wisdom Well" series of community and corporate gatherings focused on personal growth and community building. She also co-founded the Lightkeepers Collective, where she champions living systems thinking and builds a framework for an expanded network of healing and connection beyond conventional systems.

www.thelightkeeperscollective.com

Gail's Conscious Living Challenge:
Be the Change Our Medical System Desperately Needs

I love this chapter. It's full of wisdom, truth, and powerful challenges—ones I know from experience can change lives.

In 2017, I lost both of my parents to medical errors. Just writing those words brings tears to my eyes. Medical error is now the *third leading cause of death* in the United States. And yet, how many more families have to lose loved ones before we demand a better system?

I've been sounding the alarm for decades. Almost 40 years ago, when I was 17, I worked for three physicians, and I could already see the cracks. One of the physicians always had a two-hour wait. He was old-school—he didn't rush his patients through 15-minute time slots. He spent the time each one needed, and not a single patient complained. When I asked one woman why she was willing to wait so long, she said, "Because he listens to me. It's worth the wait."

I challenge you to demand the same.

Refuse to be treated like a number or a dollar sign. You deserve to be seen, heard, and treated with care.

In 2012, a National Center for Complementary and Integrative Health study[1] reported that Americans spent *$30.2 billion out-of-pocket* on complementary health approaches. That tells me loud and clear—we're not satisfied with the care we're getting. In fact, if I had my way, doctors would be paid *50% up front*, and the rest *only when you're healed*.

Over the years, I dove deep into self-education. I took courses on how to read bloodwork. I studied anatomy, facial mapping, tongue and skin diagnostics, nail health, and how pharmaceuticals deplete the body of essential vitamins and minerals. The book *Drug Muggers*[2] opened my eyes to what medications were doing at a cellular level—and before long, I had doctors asking **me** for insight.

One client brought me her bloodwork after being told everything looked "pristine." But she didn't feel pristine. I couldn't diagnose or treat her since I'm not a medical professional. But I can educate. So, I helped my client understand the difference between *clinical* reference ranges and *healthy* ones. We found **16 red flags** the doctor had overlooked—because they were within the so-called "normal" range.

Sometimes, it's too late to reverse the damage when the numbers finally fall out of range. So I challenge you:

- **Question your bloodwork.** Don't accept "you're fine" if you don't feel fine.
- **Learn the difference** between low-normal, high-normal, and truly optimal.
- **Know your own body systems** as thoroughly as you know your phone apps.

And if you work in corporate America? *I challenge you to advocate for a wellness plan.*

Ask for massage, chiropractic, and energy work.
Ask for preventative care, not just sick care.
Demand more than a prescription pad.

Meeting Sarah inspired me to reconnect with my community. I created a spiritual circle of women who meet every other month. We talk about our health, our challenges, our traumas. We uplift, support, and hold space for each other.

And one more challenge:
Step away from Zoom. Put down the phone. *Meet in person. Hug someone. Feel their energy. Share yours.* That kind of connection heals more than we know.

In *It's Time*, we open the film with Synthia Andrews' quote: *"Judgment is the only thing that separates us."* And we end with Muhammad Ali's powerful reminder: *"Service to others is the rent you pay for your room here on earth."*

Kindness matters.
Love matters.

As Sarah says so beautifully in her chapter: *"It's time to move from the love of power to the power of love."*

Watch your thoughts. They shape your reality.

As Henry Ford said, *"Whether you think you can, or think you can't—you're right."*

You can see the glass as half full or half empty... or you can throw out the glass entirely and build something new.

I've been through two divorces. I've been judged—by the church, by family, by people who didn't understand my choices. But in the end, I had two options:

Be miserable. Or be happy.
I chose happiness.
I challenge you to do the same.

1. https://www.nccih.nih.gov/news/press-releases/americans-spent-302-billion-outofpocket-on-complementary-health-approaches
2. *Drug Muggers: Which Medications Are Robbing Your Body of Essential Nutrients – and Natural Ways to Restore Them* by Suzy Cohen, RPh

6

Introducing Mona Sobhani, Ph.D.

WHEN WE WERE CASTING the experts we wanted to feature in *It's Time*, a friend recommended Dr. Mona Sobhani. I watched a few of her podcast interviews and was impressed by how she expressed herself—not just as a neuroscientist but as someone who brought a spiritual lens to science and life. That blend really resonated with me.

I reached out to Mona, and the connection was easy. She was interested and aligned with our vision, and everything flowed perfectly for her trip to Sedona, Arizona, where we were filming.

As it turns out, Sandie Sedgbeer already knew her—of course. (At this point, I'm convinced Sandie knows just about everyone.)

One of the things that struck me about Mona was her backstory. She had walked away from a traditional scientific career because her findings didn't fit the narrative advertisers and investors wanted to support. Her work was being suppressed—and rather than compromise her integrity, she chose to leave. That alone says a lot about Mona's integrity.

But she shared something else that really stayed with me—her experience of how the education system disconnected her from her spiritual self and her relationship with Source. That hit home for me.

Having observed that pattern myself, hearing Mona voice it so clearly was like a lightbulb moment. It confirmed what I had sensed for a long time. I went to school for thirteen years, trying to get a real education. I kept switching schools and majors, looking for something meaningful, something practical, something I could actually use in my life.

Eventually, I realized—it's a game. So, I got my degrees, checked the boxes, and then got serious about learning what really mattered: from authors I respected, podcasts with experts, and conversations that lit me up. No matter how compelling they sound, I've never believed in following just one expert. I want to hear from many. I want to gather information and perspectives and then piece together what resonates *for me*.

Anyone who claims to have all the answers is a walking red flag. That's not clarity — that's ego.

When Two Worlds Collide: A Neuroscientist's Accidental Spiritual Awakening

by Mona Sobhani, Ph.D.

Whenever I speak at events, I start by announcing, "I am the least likely person to tell the story of spiritual transformation." Here's why.

As one might expect of a traditionally trained cognitive neuroscientist, I was a scientific materialist whose philosophy and worldview were predicated on the belief that reality is composed of just physical matter. That's what they train us to believe in neuroscience graduate school. I was also taught that the universe has no external meaning—that everything is random and all meaning is created by our brains. "Our brains are coincidence detectors, so they look for coincidences and then create meaning and stories," our professors taught. It's a standard view among scientists. This was the indoctrination we received in graduate school, and we believed it, without understanding that other philosophies and world views also describe reality.

My heritage is Persian, and Persians are indigenously Zoroastrian, based on the teachings of the Iranian prophet Zoroaster (also known as Zarathustra), which is estimated to have originated as early as 4,000 years ago. Many rituals and traditions run through my culture. But growing up in America, I was never very spiritual or religious, even though my mother and grandmother both practiced a form of divination using coffee grinds. To me, it was just something they did for relatives and friends at family gatherings to intuit things about their past, present, and future. Since I didn't really understand it, I ignored it, telling myself that science was my religion. Until I started going home on the weekends during graduate school when my mother would insist on reading for me. She would tell me specific and very private things about my life that later came true. I tried to ignore that, too, because I couldn't explain any of it with my science.

Science is a bit of a cult in that it's difficult to express views that go against the mainstream for fear of losing your colleagues, respect, and your job. I did my best to keep those two parts of my life separate. My education and training did an excellent job of disconnecting me from being connected. And it worked well for a while . . . until it didn't. Then life became increasingly difficult. After a while, the cognitive dissonance of believing one thing that made sense to me and seeing the evidence of something else that I couldn't refute but couldn't make sense of triggered an existential crisis.

Every morning, I would wake up with one question on my mind: "Why are we here?" Unable to answer it, my attention moved into unexplored territory. From being focused solely on my scientific worldview and my work, my mind was being pulled toward the familial aspect of my cultural heritage, and how we incorporate divination, ritual, and tradition into our lives.

As my two worlds began to collide, I started to experience a series of coincidences and synchronicities that were difficult to explain statistically. I was a rational, logical thinker and trained to be a reductionist. This struggle caused a lot of mental anguish, a deep sense of inner conflict and confusion. On the one hand, beginning to see meaning in life and the universe opened me up to mystical aspects. On the other, my scientific training and indoctrination had become the core of my identity, which I had worked hard to build over all my years of study. The only way to cope was to resist all thoughts and acceptance of metaphysics, spirituality, and anything that mainstream science could not explain. Such things were a betrayal of science and who I thought I was. They diminished me and made me feel foolish and less valuable.

But the gate had been opened, and I couldn't shut it now. I started to recall how, as a child and a teenager, I had experienced precognitive dreams. I'd been so connected to the flow of life, always seeming to know when something was about to happen or the right moment to email or call someone. As I grew older and started immersing myself in science, I disconnected from that part of me. But now, suddenly, the precognitive dreams, intuitions, and inexplicable inner knowing all came flooding back. And I wasn't dealing with it very well. Instead of surrendering, I was resisting. My mind was a fortress, built on the principles of science and reason, and I was not ready to let in anything that did not fit within those walls.

Then, one night, I listened to a non-spiritual podcast hosted by the comedian Chelsea Handler, who happened to have a psychic medium called Laura Lynn Jackson on the show. Knowing that Chelsea was a skeptic, I was intrigued. Laura described the spiritual framework she believed in, which included concepts such as karma, soul lessons, and multiple reincarnations, and explained how we choose our lives and our life lessons. When she mentioned the book *Many Lives, Many Masters* by the Yale and Columbia-educated psychiatrist Dr. Brian Weiss, which was written as an orthodox case study, I immediately ordered it. When it arrived, I was surprised to find that it was about "past life regression." I had never heard of it.

That was the beginning for me. I took the book seriously, and read more of Dr. Weiss's work, which led me to other books on past life regression and healing modalities. I was fascinated, because as a neuroscientist, I know that Western medicine had very few options to address mental health concerns and chronic ailments. I started interviewing behavioral health practitioners who used past life regression in their practices and scientists to get their perspectives and understanding of what they thought they were doing and if they were actually healing people. I wanted to know if they genuinely believed there was a spiritual dimension to what they were doing, or if it was all fantasy or a placebo effect.

Feeling a little crazy, as if I was losing my identity, and wondering about the spiritual beliefs of other scientists, I also started to interview colleagues that I had known over ten years but had never discussed such things. I was astonished to find that many of them were very open-minded. We discussed how the true spirit of science is to be curious and open-minded, to follow the evidence, and to accept that if something happens even once, it's not a data point that one can ignore. Through these conversations with my colleagues and other professionals, the idea that there's "something here" and that science needed to update its models began solidifying for me.

I realized I had really been looking for meaning on this journey, but as a scientist, I wanted absolute proof that somebody had found concrete evidence for it and a way to define "meaning."

Dr. Brian Weiss says in his books that the meaning of life is to enjoy all the small moments, like pouring yourself a cup of coffee or enjoying the way the morning light streams into your room. Just the little things. That simple psychological reframe profoundly changed me. Suddenly, the little moments in my life started to have meaning. I found corroboration in various literature about the relationality of humans and the importance of our relationships. I had lost sight of that during my crisis. And the moment I started to incorporate those actions and philosophies into my daily living, the quality of my life significantly improved.

Now many of science's more significant questions began to make sense. For example, the idea of the holographic universe resonated deeply, because it ties together all the different modalities within spirituality and metaphysics that we have a hard time explaining with reductionist science. Reductionist science separates things—we divide them into separate concepts and constructs with labels. But that's not how nature is. Everything is interconnected and related. Everything is systems. So, the way we currently do science doesn't even make sense. The idea of a hologram where all the pieces are connected and seeing humans as a microcosm of the universe's macrocosm makes a lot more sense. It addresses life from a systems perspective, so when one thing is affected, everything else is affected. That really is how things are in nature and in the universe.

Then there are the questions of energy and consciousness, which are tough topics in science because these words have different meanings in the spiritual space versus the science space. In neuroscience, we define consciousness and study it mainly from the perspective of our everyday waking consciousness—i.e., perception, attention, focus, etc. That's what we analyze, and it's still the most complex problem in science. It's so difficult for science to map other states of consciousness. We don't have a good understanding of how consciousness could emerge from physical matter. There's a constant debate, and we are still fumbling to find the neural correlates. We assume it comes from the brain, that somehow our neurons firing together make this emergent property of consciousness, and even that is up for debate. But when you zoom out of science and return to the human experience, we have a variety of conscious experiences—sleeping, dreaming, the state between being awake and being asleep, psychedelic, meditative, and trance states—that science never looks at. But that's what you start to see in the spiritual perspective, which is more focused on the entire human experience than defining and understanding the concept of ordinary waking consciousness and its neural correlates. So, there's a vast discrepancy in how we talk about these two fields.

As for "energy," science usually just associates it with ATP, like us, burning what we consider energy. Yet it has a very different definition in spiritual space, where the word is used to describe things that we can't measure and that mainstream science doesn't even define as energy because it's not on the electromagnetic spectrum.

Some theoretical physicists and cosmologists are still arguing about the exact nature of reality and the universe. Others say the universe is conscious or has some intelligence behind it. This has not been taken seriously over the past few decades but is now a more widely accepted theory. It goes back to the idea of the holographic universe. If there's intelligence in one piece, there's probably intelligence in all the pieces.

The implications of the scientific materialist paradigm ignoring spirituality are enormous. For starters, it means we are not mapping the entirety of reality. We are only mapping a subsection, which means all our models are wrong. So, a lot of our science doesn't explain phenomena well. We could say that's because we're not including the entirety of human experience, and if we did, we would have a better understanding and more complete explanations of reality.

Another important consideration is that from a humanistic perspective, believing the universe to be random, meaningless, and without purpose is unhealthy. Even if we took evolutionary theory seriously and agreed that humans developed our propensity to need spirituality or religion as a coping mechanism, we should not dismiss it if it helped us get to this point. It's unhelpful and even harmful to remove that spiritual aspect of our reality; to think that there is no purpose to life extinguishes the fire in our hearts and souls and our vitality—the very things we bring to this life experience that ignite us.

We've relied on scientific evidence for the past 50-100 years. We see it in our language, where the phrases "evidence-backed," "science-backed," and "data-driven" are ubiquitous. The problem is we don't have all the evidence because there isn't enough funding to provide it. So, saying that we're only going to focus on things that are "data-driven" or "science-backed" means we are immediately putting everything into a small box of what has been studied and what has not. Nobody seems to understand how dangerous that is for our society. We must expand what we accept as evidence to encompass other forms—empirical knowledge, personal experience, etc. From a scientific perspective—especially from a neuroscience perspective—we only have our subjective, conscious experience, which is the only way we truly know anything. So, we also need to expand our definition of knowledge because, as helpful as scientific knowledge is, it doesn't capture everything. There are qualities we cannot measure with science, things we cannot reduce to parts, and systems that, when broken apart and measured in small pieces, no longer tell the whole story.

From Traditional Science to the Science of Psychedelics

After my spiritual awakening, normal science—the kind I was used to—became too difficult for me. Knowing that I could no longer stay in the field of digital health, I started my own consulting company, working with tech companies with a more open-minded approach. I also started writing about psychedelics to spread the latest findings that showed miraculous healing in the mental health arena. The evidence of improvements in anxiety, depression, PTSD, eating disorders, and alcohol and substance dependence was compelling, and I wanted to find other scientists who were also open-minded or spiritually curious about our reality.

Psychedelic research is fundamental. It's expanding science in many ways, especially our understanding of consciousness. I found a collaborator, and we organized spin-off events at our annual Society for Neuroscience Conference, one of which was on neuroscience and spirituality. We also started researching the possibilities of creating events around alternative models of consciousness, bringing scientists together to explore topics such as "What do we really understand about our reality?" "How can we bridge science and spirituality?" and "How do we feel about consciousness?" "We wanted to create safe spaces where scientists could explore these questions together.

Psychedelics put you into an altered state of consciousness, which is different than your ordinary waking consciousness. They thin the line between your conscious and subconscious mind. You become more receptive to information from other planes of your psychology or reality, allowing insights to pour through. There is a rumor, which has not been proven, that the English molecular biologist, biophysicist, and neuroscientist Francis Crick, who, together with James Watson, played a crucial role in deciphering the helical structure of the DNA molecule, had the idea for the double helix structure of DNA while on an LSD trip. Crick would not be alone. Many scientists have used altered states of consciousness to gain epiphanies and insights; all the best ones know where true creativity comes from.

The experiences people have in altered states of consciousness can be very healing. Many people report receiving messages or information from somebody who has passed away. Others say they felt a telepathic connection with a therapist in the room or could feel other's emotions and saw things that later came to pass. These so-called "paranormal," "anomalous," or emergent experiences that happen with psychedelics have been mainly ignored in the scientific context, dismissed as hallucinations or delusion because "it should not be possible to get information from another space/time location." It may not be "possible," but it is happening. The evidence is piling up. As more research is conducted within the context of research-designed studies, more scientists are beginning to question our understanding of reality and consciousness and our model and knowledge of illness. How can substances that primarily address serotonin or one or two neurotransmitters cure so many different diseases? They're starting to wonder, maybe it's not just about chemistry, but how chemicals are expressed in behavior or psychology? Moving into these altered states of consciousness allows our body to access information it can use to heal itself.

Of course, it's essential to add that psychedelics are not the only avenue for altering one's state of consciousness. Breathwork, meditation, and trance states are other easy-access ways to expand one's consciousness and achieve similar effects to those you get with psychedelics.

What attracts me about psychedelic research is what happens in that liminal space between one state of consciousness and a higher state. That is the space where rationality meets creativity. We all do a lot of rational, logical thinking and we all know—many scientists included—that when we let go and take a walk, a nap, or meditate, answers come to problems that we could not resolve before. Indeed, I have found through my personal journey and research that the answers to interpersonal questions and issues are more likely to arise in that space.

So, in expanding our understanding of consciousness and neuroscience, this psychedelic renaissance is proving to be an essential part of the revolution that's starting to happen. I think it's going to be especially useful in the medical arena, where it has been so challenging to find solutions to mental, emotional, and psychological conditions, addictions, and challenging health conditions.

The agendas of science are driven by what gets funded, which in the United States is decided mainly by the National Science Foundation and the National Institutes for Health. Until now, medicine has been focused on pharmaceuticals, which are chemical substrates, so that's where all the funding has gone. But times are changing, and there are other modalities that can improve health and healing in humans that address different parts of our biological systems. Looking ahead, I think our approach to medicine will drastically change. I believe that sound, light, frequency, sacred geometry, and many other modalities not yet adequately examined or incorporated into medicine will start coming to the fore. We need to start focusing on the entire aspect of a human, not just the chemical. We are electrochemical magnetic beings. Electrical currents have magnetic fields. And as we increase our knowledge of the science of frequency and vibration, we will be able to leverage those in healing.

There is little doubt that humanity is at a significant turning point. We have moved away from our true nature, disconnecting from each other and the land. But you can only move away from your biological nature for so long before things start to break apart. We have the potential to make an evolutionary leap if we are willing to work on ourselves. The more work we put into ourselves, the more it will benefit us and our environment.

Humans are neurologically wired for attachment, love, connection, community, and cooperation. Why we evolved this way is a mystery. But if we take evolutionary theory seriously, it must be because it increases our odds of survival as a species. Love, connection, and attachment are critical to our health and well-being. Which is all too prevalent in societies around the world today. We are relational creatures. Whether it's our relationship with ourselves, others, or our environment, we are completely interconnected with everything. Humans and other biological organisms work more powerfully together in groups. We do not evolve alone. When we move away from that, we feel threatened and unsafe. Fear becomes difficult to suppress, and when an organism moves from a place of fear, it becomes dangerous. So, we need to address this disconnection that's come about in our society and try to reconnect people in any way possible because not feeling safe drives people towards fearful behaviors.

Looking back over my journey, I see a massive difference in me. Old me was very reductionist, a materialist, wholly focused on scientific evidence. Science was my only religion. I thought I knew everything, which was very condescending and arrogant. Unsurprisingly, I felt very separate from everything and everyone.

My journey from science to spirituality opened me up and made me more loving, more human. I no longer believe I know everything, but I do know that the world is a lot weirder than science believes, and there are so many things that we cannot measure. While the scientific method is wonderful, it's extremely limited and inadequate to address our reality.

My worldview changes daily, but I always do my best to stay open to the knowledge that the universe has a spiritual and mystic dimension. And I leave a space for the possibility that it also has intelligence. And that there are other intelligences besides us in this universe.

I also know that love is a core feature of humanity. It takes out the selfish component of behavior. It brings us together and creates supportive systems. We are driven towards love and connection; they bind us together. So, regardless of whatever lies ahead for humanity in these transitional years, I know that the answer to every question we may have lies not in science but in love.

***

MONA SOBHANI, PH.D., is a cognitive neuroscientist. A former research scientist at the University of Southern California, she holds a doctorate in neuroscience from the University of Southern California and completed a post-doctoral fellowship at Vanderbilt University with the MacArthur Foundation Law and Neuroscience Project. She was also a scholar with the Saks Institute for Mental Health Law, Policy, and Ethics and her work has been featured in the *New York Times*, *VOX*, and other media outlets.

Dr. Sobhani is the author of the Ommie 2022 Best Spiritual Book, *Proof of Spiritual Phenomena: A Neuroscientist's Discovery of the Ineffable Mysteries of the Universe*, which is also a recipient of the 2023 Scientific and Medical Network Book Prize. In the *Cosmos, Coffee, & Consciousness Substack*, she writes about science & spirituality, the psychedelic renaissance, altered states of consciousness, and the transpersonal. She is co-founder of Exploring Consciousness, a community of curious scientists who are seeking to understand consciousness, spirituality, and the nature of our reality.

https://www.monasobhaniphd.com

Gail's Conscious Living Challenge:
Question, Discern, and Stay in Love

If you've made it this far in the book, you've probably started noticing some recurring themes. Each of the contributors shares their unique lens, but there's a strong thread running through all of them: it's time to question what we've been taught.

In this chapter, I want to challenge you to take a close look at the "experts" you follow, the systems you trust, and the education you've received. Ask yourself:

- Do they really have all the answers?
- Are you relying too heavily on one perspective, one teacher, one source of information?
- Is it time to expand your field of view and start discerning what actually resonates with you?

Also, let's talk about education. For decades, we've been taught that success depends on degrees and credentials. But the world is shifting. Many companies today are placing more value on experience than on a traditional education. And let's be honest—some of the books and materials still being used in schools are wildly outdated.

Mona talks about the book *Many Lives, Many Masters*, which brings up a funny (and slightly terrifying) memory for me.

I was on a dating app and had arranged to meet a man for dinner. During our chat, he said he had bought me *Many Lives, Many Masters*—which he had supposedly left in his car. He also told me he worked for NASA. Then he asked, "If we really went to the moon, why haven't we been back?" I was intrigued. His explanation? "The beings who live inside the moon were upset that we left behind our equipment and killed a bunch of their dust mites, so they invited us not to return."

Now... whether you believe that or not is beside the point. What matters is this: it made me think differently.

That's the Real Challenge

Not to agree. Not to argue. But to listen, reflect, and if something doesn't resonate—let it go.

Anyway, after dinner, he asked me to walk with him to his car to get the book. Then he suggested we drive to a video store to rent a movie. Red flags everywhere. I politely declined, took the book, and never saw him again. Honestly, I may have narrowly avoided becoming one of those Dateline stories. But I did read the book—and I loved it.

Mona also touches on past life regression, something I've explored myself. I had a session with the late Dr. Norm Shealy, MD, and the experience blew me away. Even if you don't believe in past lives, the information that came through was undeniably relevant to my life. It made me feel seen and validated in ways I didn't expect.

If you do seek out a past life regression, make sure it's with someone truly qualified. There are people who will say whatever you want to hear or send you down a rabbit hole that leads nowhere. Be discerning. If it resonates—great. If not, toss it and move on.

I've found that some of the most profound awakenings come from the simplest things:

- The soft, cold nose of my cat touching mine.
- The awe I feel when I look at my horse, Holly—a massive, majestic creature with the heart of a gentle alien.
- A new lip balm or chapstick. Yes, really.
- The satisfying feeling of checking off tasks from my to-do list.

Those little joys matter.

I haven't personally experimented with psychedelics, though I know many who have had deeply healing experiences. For me, it's sound and light. I believe we are sound and light beings—emanating from Source, from God—and that's how I choose to connect. The ancients knew this. They used sound and light for healing, and I do the same today through the Harmonic Egg®.

When I'm in the Egg, I feel like I'm tapping into something bigger than myself—like I've entered a non-local realm, much like a controlled remote viewer. It's in that altered-yet-natural state that so many of my insights, ideas, and creative downloads come through.

Here's the truth: There is no one-size-fits-all path. You have to explore, reflect, and discern what works for you—what helps you feel empowered, aligned, and at peace.

So I'll leave you with this:

I challenge you to stay in a place of love.
Love is the highest vibration.
Fear is a very bad perfume to wear.
Embrace change.
Question everything.
And live from love. Always.

7

Introducing Charles Monroe, Jr.

CHARLES MONROE first contacted me in 2021 after learning about the Harmonic Egg®. He wanted to open a location in Maryland to support his family, friends, and local community through sound and light therapy. From our first conversation, I knew we were on the same wavelength. He wasn't just curious—he was already profoundly well-versed in sound, light, and energy medicine. Since then, Charles has become a respected voice in the Harmonic Egg community—what we lovingly call an "Egg Guardian"—bringing wisdom, heart, dedication, and grounded insight to the work. When we were casting for *It's Time*, we had already selected all our experts and weren't planning to feature any Egg owners in the film—we wanted to keep the focus broad, not biased or promotional. But then, as life would have it, one of our cast members had an accident and couldn't travel.

When Sandie asked who could step in, Charles' face popped into my mind. I hadn't even considered him... but I've learned to trust those intuitive hits.

I called him on a whim, gave him the filming dates, and—miraculously—he had already booked time off for a vacation... with no concrete plans. Well, he did now!.

He showed up, gave a phenomenal interview, and brought a grounded, powerful energy to the film. While we didn't include his thoughts about the Egg in the final cut to keep things focused, we did film a special **BONUS segment** with him, which includes that conversation—and, let's just say, Charles and I had an unforgettable adventure with the bees. You'll have to watch to understand.

Your Body Knows How to Heal Itself
by Charles Monroe, Jr.

In 2018, a highly respected and award-winning consultant cardiologist based in London published an article in The Guardian newspaper, claiming that modern medicine is a major threat to public health. "Most patients," the cardiologist pronounced, "will derive no health improvement from medication. We should tackle the root causes of disease instead." [1]

For centuries, long before we had doctors, every culture across the globe relied on nature, plants, home remedies, and traditional healers—i.e., medicine men, shamans, wise women, and hedge witches—to heal their physical, mental, and spiritual ailments. Then, in the early 1900s, modern medicine began to take over. For the next 200 years, we saw tremendous breakthrough advances in medicine—from surgical techniques and vaccines that controlled infectious diseases to the discovery of natural compounds in plants that offered endless possibilities for drug development.

Then, a significant shift occurred. Progress accelerated, technology began to reshape our world, and life started to speed up. In just a few decades, we transitioned from room-sized computers to multifunctional devices that fit our pockets and dominate our daily lives. Technology opened up the world and revolutionized every aspect of our lives, from business, education, and healthcare to what we do in our downtime. Before we knew it, the root causes of ill health also shifted from primarily external threats like transmissible diseases to lifestyle-driven conditions. Stress has become the leading cause of illness, and the roots of poor health have increasingly become an inside job.

But despite thousands of years of human evolution, one thing has never changed: just like all things in nature, our bodies know how to heal themselves. They always have, and they always will. Break a bone, and a doctor will realign those bones, wrap them up, and set you up for success. But they will not regrow and heal them for you. Only your body can do that job.

An analogy I use with my clients is to have them imagine for a moment that they are a great artist known for painting beautiful works of art. Then, somehow, they got distracted or lost interest and stopped painting until a friend came along and reminded them how great they were and inspired them to start producing their masterpieces again. Their friend is not responsible for the new paintings. All their friend did was have a conversation with them. The client could paint all along. Their friend just gave them a little pep talk, a nudge.

Modern medicine has the tools and knowledge to identify what's wrong and perform mechanical repairs with various pharmaceuticals. But it cannot heal your body for you. Graze your knee, and your skin will heal. Cut your finger, and platelets in your body will clot to stop the bleeding, white cells will remove the dead, injured cells, and new healthy cells will repair the damaged tissue. Your body is designed to maintain homeostasis, and every cell in your body is a dynamic, living unit that is constantly monitoring, adjusting, and working to restore itself according to the original DNA code that created it.

Health is our most precious asset, and nature is our most precious resource. With its emphasis on treating symptoms rather than looking at the root cause of a symptom or condition, modern medicine has effectively brainwashed us into discounting thousands of years of knowledge and wisdom. However, with scientific discoveries now showing that the variety of methods employed by our ancestors are natural forms of energy healing, science, and medicine are finally beginning to rethink their attitude to health and wellbeing.

What Modern Medicine Can Learn From the Past

Energy therapies have been used since ancient times. These methods of healing afflictions of the body and spirit are part of Asian healing practices like acupuncture, yoga, and Qigong, which all operate on the principle that illness results from blockages or imbalances in our body's life force energy. The Chinese refer to this unseen energy as Chi or Qi. The Hawaiians call it Mana. The Sanskrit word for it is Prana. In the West, it's been referred to by various names, including orgone, ether, entelechy, animal magnetism, and psychic energy. Regardless, all energy therapies employ frequency to unblock or rebalance that vital life force energy.

Energy is a fundamental constant of the universe—it exists everywhere in all forms and cannot be created or destroyed, only transformed. All living and non-living entities comprise the same energy, which travels through various electromagnetic waves like heat, light, sound, and color. We are composed of a multidimensional mix of vibrating energies that constantly change based on our moods, physical health, what we eat and drink, and even what we think and feel. This dynamic is true for every organ and system in our bodies. Although science does not fully understand how this happens, it can now measure that our thoughts and emotions are constantly transmitted beyond our bodies to others through these energy fields.

Energy's primary role is to make things happen and to create change. To do this, it must remain in motion. The more cycles energy completes in one second, the higher its frequency. When the vibration slows down, energy becomes physical matter that appears solid. For example, when we remove energy from water by lowering its temperature, the molecules slow down until they form solid matter—specifically, ice, which is dense and heavy. Conversely, if we raise the temperature of ice, its molecular vibration accelerates, eventually turning it back into liquid water. If we continue to increase the temperature, the water will boil and transform into steam, which is weightless, formless, and nearly invisible to the naked eye.

A healthy human body has a vibrational frequency range of 62-70 MHz. When the frequency of your cells drops below 62MHz, they will start to change or mutate, allowing illness to set in. Humans are meant to be fluid like water, not dense like sludge or solid like ice. Energy must flow freely within, through, and around us if we want to remain healthy.

Cymatics

The word "cymatics" comes from the Greek word "sima," which means "wave." Cymatics studies how the visible effects of vibrations and sounds affect matter. Water vibrates to the frequencies in sounds; since your body is made mainly of water, sound will profoundly affect it. Sound is a carrier for information; hence, it's an excellent delivery mechanism for intention.

Masaru Emoto conducted many experiments to show how intention affects water. In some, he would use frozen water; in others, he would use plants. On two pieces of paper, he would write down the words "I love you" and "I hate you" and place them in two separate pots with the plants. Both plants would receive the same amount of sunlight and plant food, and he would say the words aloud daily. Since plants don't have ears, they cannot hear us but receive and respond to information.

This is borne out by an article published on the California Academy of Sciences website, which reported, "Plants are surprising organisms—without brains and central nervous systems, they are still able to sense the environment that surrounds them. Plants can perceive light, scent, touch, wind, and even gravity and they respond to sounds, too." The article, which shared the results of experiments conducted by scientists at the University of Missouri, concluded that plants respond to vibrations. In short, our thoughts and intentions carry frequencies. Frequencies carry information. The water in the plants vibrates to the information carried on those frequencies, and the plants, in turn, respond.[2]

Masaru Emoto's research suggests that our emotions, words, and vibrations—along with those of the people around us—can alter the composition of the water molecules in our bodies. Negative thoughts and emotions adversely affect our bodies' water molecules and, consequently, our wellbeing, while positive thoughts and emotions have a beneficial impact.

Research has scientifically demonstrated that sound can create mandala-like patterns in physical matter. In the same way that a pebble thrown into a still pond creates ripples that spread outward in all directions, sound waves propagate from their source as they travel through the air. Likewise, when objects underwater vibrate, they generate sound-pressure waves that compress and decompress the water molecules as the sound wave travels through the sea.

Cymatics demonstrates the influence sound frequencies have on our minds and bodies. It illustrates how specific sound waves can generate intricate geometric patterns in various materials, including water, which makes up a significant portion of our bodies. Using sound frequencies, cymatic therapy promotes cell coherence and enhances overall wellbeing. The vibrations from cymatic therapy devices—such as gongs, singing bowls, didgeridoos, and drums—engage our cells, prompting them to resonate at their natural, healthy frequencies. Their benefits extend well beyond physical wellness, significantly enhancing our mental and emotional health. Studies indicate that specific sound frequencies can effectively reduce stress and anxiety by facilitating relaxation and mental clarity, lowering our cortisol levels, and increasing our blood flow to help alleviate anxiety and depression, restore balance and harmony in our body, and enhance our immune system.

Sound can also evoke concepts and pictures in our minds, allowing us to transform them into mental imagery. Sanskrit, the oldest language in the world, employs sound to shape and reprogram the subconscious mind. This practice, known as Shabda Yoga, or the Yoga of Sound, involves using mantras, which can be seed sounds, words, or short Sanskrit phrases. Their power is said to lie in the energetic and auditory vibrations of the words and the intention behind the sounds and syllables.

The Magic of Sound

We have a tradition of blessing our food. Have you ever wondered why we do that? A blessing is a prayer asking for divine protection, a small favor, or a gift from the heavens. Blessing our food is both an intention and a prayer in that we are not only giving thanks for the food itself but also setting an intention that it provides the healthy nourishment our bodies need. Food contains a lot of water, and the energy in our intention reconfigures the water's frequencies, bringing it into balance with our bodies.

We only have to think back to the last time we ate in a busy restaurant to recall the mix of energies in the room, with some diners happily celebrating or good-naturedly waiting for their meals to arrive. In contrast, others likely looked hungry, tired, and stressed, especially if their meal took longer than anticipated. It doesn't take much to imagine what the kitchen must have been like, with chefs and trainees rushing around to produce several meals simultaneously. We rarely give much thought to the frequencies of all those invisibly circulating sounds and intentions being absorbed right into the water in our food and then transferred into our bodies. Yet it is happening all the time. How do we counteract that? We say a silent prayer. Or we hold our hands above the table and silently visualize reiki energy bathing our plate. With a blessing, we use love and grace to transform the lower frequencies from those sounds, energies, and intentions. Blessing our food is far more than a custom; it's an act of physical transformation that works by entrainment and is backed up by science. Sound is a carrier for information and a delivery mechanism for intention. This is why it is such an effective form of energy healing. Light and color are two other forms of energy healing that work by entrainment.

Entrainment is the tendency for two oscillating bodies to lock into phase so they vibrate in harmony. One way this is taught in physics is by placing several grandfather clocks in a room with their pendulums independently swinging back and forth at their own pace and rate. Then, a large grandfather clock is brought into the room. Every clock will synchronize with the large grandfather clock within a couple of days. This demonstrates how a strong and powerful vibrating source can influence a weaker vibrating force. It's called rhythmic entrainment.

The law of entrainment is the basis of sound healing therapy when applied to the human body. It works like this: Your body is designed to seek and maintain homeostasis. Each chakra in your body corresponds to a different note. If a chakra is out of balance, it can be brought back into balance or returned to homeostasis by entrainment—i.e., by playing a note or even a song in the same key as the note of the chakra. So, for example, if I found that a client's root chakra was out of balance, I would use a singing bowl or a tuning fork tuned to the note C. This note would play the role of the grandfather clock—the dominant frequency—that would entrain the root chakra and bring it back to homeostasis. Color and light respond in the same way. The difference lies in how sound and light influence the chakras; sound involves air molecules moving at specific frequencies, while light uses photons. This can affect your emotions, which, like your chakras, also are part of your electromagnetic field. In fact, anything that affects your electromagnetic field, whether physical or psychological, will influence your chakras and emotions.

Instruments have served as health devices for centuries. The didgeridoo was used as a medicinal tool by the Aborigines in Australia, as were drums, which had been utilized long before the advent of traditional medicine. Aside from working on the lower chakras, drums were used for communication and healing. Shamans would carefully select the people to be trained as drummers because a lot was required of them. Their life would be totally different from their fellows; they needed to live differently, eat differently, and sleep separately from the rest of their community. Tending their energy was a matter of great importance because a shaman's energy and the intention of whatever they would be sharing would be imbued into their instrument and transmitted to the rest of the community at large whenever they played their drum.

Thoughts Are Electric, and Emotions (and Intentions) Are Magnetic

Our thoughts and our intentions play a critical role in healing. We are electromagnetic beings. Hence, I always tell my clients that when you set an intention, you literally create a timeline. They must imbue that intention with feeling to make themselves a vibrational match for that timeline. Certain scriptures in the Bible speak about this when they say, "Pray as if you already have it," which means, "Feel what you would feel if you already had it."

In today's medicine, everything is about symptoms. This is how physicians arrive at their diagnoses. However, while I will listen to my client's symptoms in my wellness practice, I am looking for the root because that is what ultimately needs healing.

Here's an example from one of my client's cases.

Jean came to me just before she was about to have her gallbladder removed. A sonogram had revealed a mass in her gallbladder. When I scanned Jean with the BioWell device, it showed me that her body was sending a lot of energy into her liver, which is closely related to the gallbladder. In Chinese medicine, the liver is where we store anger and resentment.

So, I asked Jean, "Who are you angry at?"

Jean told me she had gotten divorced some months before and was still very resentful and angry at her former husband. It wasn't difficult to work out what had happened. Jean's emotions had compromised her bile and liver, allowing cholesterol to build up and accumulate in the reservoir of her gallbladder, which had eventually solidified into gallstones.

When I explained the connection between her disposition and her physical liver (which is not always easy for clients to accept), Jean understood that to heal her body, she first needed to heal her emotions. We agreed on a course of six sessions, the first four of which were designed to work on the symptoms by reducing the pain and fortifying the bile and liver, after which we would focus on the root cause. I put Jean on a celery juice regimen and used frequency healing in the form of drumming and rattles to break up the gallstones. After applying the specific frequency of the drums and rattles to break up Jean's gallstones, we then canceled out the frequencies of the emotions of anger and resentment with an opposing frequency that was 180 degrees out of phase with her original emotions. This is similar to how noise cancellation headphones work, where ambient noise is picked up by a tiny microphone in the headphones and then played back in real time, 180 degrees out of phase to cancel itself out. This is precisely what happens when dealing with thoughts and emotions because thoughts are electric, and emotions are magnetic. At the end of the first four sessions, Jean's CT scans showed a significant reduction in the size of several large gallstones down to a tiny, five-millimeter stone. With that reduction accomplished, we then turned our attention to the root cause of Jean's ailment, which, because it involved anger and resentment, required her to work on forgiveness. As Jean's father was half Hawaiian, we used a musical track featuring the native Hawaiian ho'opono pono practice and prayer, with which she was already familiar.

Ho'opono pono is a Hawaiian prayer or mantra whose words—"I am sorry. Please forgive me. I love you. I am grateful,"—are repeated several times. The higher frequencies of love imbued into the words of the mantra affect the body's water, which in turn affects the energy field of the person reciting the prayer.

When Jean next visited her doctor, he was thrilled to find that she no longer needed surgery and asked if he could meet me to learn more about what we had done.

Balancing Your Biofield

The human body is surrounded by a subtle electrical field known as the biofield, which consists of electricity emissions and biophotons—light that all living things naturally emit. Under the right conditions, our bodies possess an innate ability to heal themselves. However, energy must flow in, through, and around us to maintain good health. Stagnant energy can disrupt this flow, leading to imbalances that may result in illness. According to Deepak Chopra, when a person's biofield is out of balance, it is possible to restore harmony by directly addressing it.

The Harmonic Egg is a totally unique resonance chamber that utilizes sacred geometry, light, color, and sound frequencies to restore and rebalance the biofield by promoting deep relaxation and well-being in the physical body. Bio-healing energy envelops the client inside the Egg's chamber, enabling the sound and light frequencies to create a unique and transformative mind-body connection.

Among our clients are many holistic healers and naturopaths who find that the Harmonic Egg is a reliable way to replenish spiritual health when they begin feeling depleted. This approach offers our clients a unique holistic healing and spiritual rejuvenation experience, and helps them better understand their wellbeing, ultimately supporting their journey toward optimal spiritual, mental, and physical health.

Clients tell us that they have experienced relief from the hypervigilance of PTSD and from career, relationship, and health-related stress and anxiety. Those who have experienced physical trauma often carry stress in their bodies as muscle memory. Because the Harmonic Egg is a no-touch modality, it seems to provide more relief than other modalities for these clients.

When clients ask me how it works, I use the examples of tuning forks and singing bowls to help them understand the human energy field—their biofield—the external factors that can affect it, and how these factors can manifest psychologically, emotionally, and physically as blockages or "areas of stuck energy" in their physical, emotional, or mental bodies. Ancient Chinese and Hindu medicine used the meridians of acupuncture and chakras to explain how blocked or unbalanced biofield energy can result in physical or spiritual illness. I explain how the frequencies of light, sound, color, and the sacred geometry utilized in the Egg's unique construction combine to create a fertile environment to facilitate healing.

But there's more to it than that. Gail Lynn, the brilliant inventor of the Harmonic Egg®, regards every session as a co-creative process. The construction of the Egg is one part, and the client's intention to experience health and wellbeing is another. The third part is provided by the level of consciousness and energy of the person facilitating the client's experience in the Egg. Considering what I wrote about the power of thoughts, prayers, and intentions, the person overseeing the client's experience must do their due diligence. I take this very seriously and strictly monitor my consciousness and energy levels. I've also learned that I couldn't have been better trained for my current work. My knowledge of the correlation between the frequencies of sound, light, and color gathered over years of experience and study has enabled me to develop the skill of intuiting the precise music and colors each client needs in their sessions so that, together, all three of us—the client, the Egg, and me, are united in our intention to facilitate the client's return to homeostasis and well-being.

I know that caring professionals have the same goal for their patients. But bringing all these components together is more complicated for today's physicians and healthcare workers than it used to be. Today's physicians are not encouraged to combine their intuition with their clinical knowledge and expertise when making diagnoses or to recommend complementary therapies and treatments that might support a patient's recovery for fear of a malpractice suit if something goes wrong. It's hard to believe that some doctors in the past were so familiar with the art of sound healing that a set of tuning forks was a necessary part of their healing toolkit. But I've heard of several. Contrast that with what people might think or say today if their doctor pulled out a roll of tuning forks instead of writing a prescription! It's not difficult to gauge how far medicine has strayed from the spirit of its origins over the last two centuries as our obsession with science caused us to (almost) forget that medicine is also an art.

To conclude this chapter on a positive note, I believe there are two reasons why modern medicine has the potential for change.

First, at their core, every doctor and healthcare professional is a healer. Whether consciously or unconsciously, the drive to heal the sick, alleviate pain, and save lives is what motivated them to pursue this path. And second, we are fortunate to live in an era where science is increasingly recognizing that everything in our universe, and beyond, is composed of energy, and that nothing occurs in isolation. For as Dr. Jude Currivan, a cosmologist, planetary healer, futurist, author, and co-founder of WholeWorld-View.org, discusses in her short documentary *A Radical Guide to Reality*:

> "Scientific breakthroughs and evidence at all scales of existence are converging with universal wisdom teachings to reveal that our entire universe meaningfully exists and purposefully evolves as an interdependent and unified entity, inviting us to re-member who we really are—and who we can evolve to become.
>
> "With scientifically-based evidence we've never had before, it is time for a fragmented worldview based on the illusion of separation to end. Healing our understanding offers us an experiential and transformative pathway home to our innate wholeness and offers us authentic hope for a future that works for the good of the whole".[3]

1. *https://www.theguardian.com/society/2018/aug/30/modern-medicine-major-threat-public-health*

2. *https://www.calacademy.org/explore-science/do-plants-hear*

3. *A Radical Guide to Reality* short documentary: *https://www.youtube.com/watch?v=6GkLM8o4RXc*

CHARLES MONROE, JR. is the founder of ChromoCymatics Wellness, a reiki practitioner, and a deejay. From early childhood, he was a dedicated audiophile. Sound and music were so important to him that he chose to pursue a dual major in audio technology and electrical engineering from American University and University of Maryland, College Park respectively. Growing up, Charles was also very drawn to esoteric studies and was a big fan of the works of Joseph Campbell, Manly P. Hall and Paschal Beverly Randolph. But it never occurred to him that these two interests would one day converge.

On graduating from college, Charles founded an internet consulting company, which designed some of the internet's first websites in the mid 90's like the March Of Dimes, European Union, American Society For MicroBiology, and many more. In 2003, he merged his love of music and deejaying with his web skills to start his own online radio station, which is still streaming 22 years later with close to 40 deejays streaming 24/7. For over 20 years Charles has deejayed at clubs and festivals all over the world.

In 2021, after visiting a Harmonic Egg® center in South Carolina, Charles not only opened his own healing Center, called ChromoCymatics Wellness in Maryland, but also found himself enjoying a whole new career and appearing on Talk TV/Radio shows and podcasts, sharing his prodigious knowledge of frequency technology, vibrational healing, and sound, light, and color, which he has long believed will play a critical role in the future of medicine.

https://chromocymatics.com

Gail's Conscious Living Challenge:
Be the Healer You've Been Waiting For

Charles' chapter serves as a powerful reminder: healing begins within you. So here's my challenge to you, inspired by his wisdom:

One Act of Self-Care a Day: Set a goal to perform one small, intentional act each day to reduce stress and enhance your well-being. This could be a walk in nature, five minutes of deep breathing, listening to calming music, or simply closing your eyes in stillness. Healing doesn't require a complete life overhaul; it starts with consistent, small moments of self-care.

Bless Your Food: Charles encourages us to bless our food before eating. Speak to it. Thank it, and acknowledge the energy and effort that went into its creation. This simple act transforms eating into a sacred exchange—raising your frequency and deepening your connection to what nourishes you.

No One Is Coming to Heal You: It's a powerful truth: no healer, medicine, or modality can "fix" you. Healing is an inside job. You must want it and show up for it. The tools are available, but you must do the work.

Not All Healers Are Clear: It's important to recognize that not every healer is truly a healer. Some may carry unresolved energy that can interfere with your healing journey. Be discerning and trust your instincts. A true healer dedicates themselves to the path—it's not a part-time gig or a title you can simply claim or purchase.

There's a reason traditional shamans didn't practice until they stopped bleeding; wisdom comes through life experience, self-mastery, and time. This isn't a criticism of young healers—it's a call to depth, clarity, and integrity.

Remember, Everything Is Energy

Music carries the energy of the musician. Inventions hold the intent and energy of their creators. Rocks are more than minerals—they embody the consciousness of the universe.

We weren't born into this world, we emerged from it. Just as trees grow leaves, the universe grows people.

You are not separate from nature, nor are you separate from the Source. We are all connected.

Heal Your Emotions to Heal Your Body: Unprocessed emotions create dissonance in the body.
  Grief, anger, shame, and resentment do not disappear when ignored; they root themselves in your cells and can manifest in physical ways.
  To heal your body, begin with your heart. Face the emotion, feel it, and then let it go.

You are not broken and you are not alone, but you are responsible: Healing is available—but you have to choose it.

So today, choose one thing.
Then do it again tomorrow, and the day after that.

That's how healing happens.

8

Introducing Deborah Cambio

DEBORAH CAMBIO is a holistic healing facilitator who guides individuals through physical and emotional challenges using a variety of energy-based modalities. Her approach integrates chakra balancing, color therapy, sound therapy, and other intuitive techniques to help clients realign with their true potential and purpose.

I first met Deborah through her wonderful husband, Steven Ross. We connected instantly, and she became a much-treasured friend over many shared meals and deep conversations. Yet, despite my careful considerations for casting the movie, it never occurred to me to include Deborah—until fate intervened most unexpectedly.

We had been filming at the World Research Foundation's headquarters in Sedona, Arizona. Deborah and Steven had generously allowed us to transform their space into a film set. We had just wrapped filming Dr. Mona Sobhani's contribution and were in the kitchen chatting while the crew prepared for the next expert interview.

The conversation naturally turned to energy healing and Deborah's work. She was explaining how, time and time again, she has seen people ignore the subtle signals their bodies give them until they reach a crisis point, often in the form of chronic illness, when she said something that stopped me in my tracks: "If you don't listen to the whispers, you get the nudges. And if you don't listen to the nudges, you get the hammer."

Her words hit home with undeniable clarity. It was a profound truth that resonated with my personal experience and the heart of the film's message.

"Oh, my gosh, you have to say that on film," I blurted out.

Deborah's face mirrored my own shock and excitement. How had I not thought of inviting Deborah before? With her extensive knowledge, vast toolkit of energy-healing practices, and deep intuitive wisdom, Deborah had to be part of the film.

I also realized we needed to show Deborah's work in action. The crew agreed. So, with a quick change of clothes and a touch of makeup, Deborah stepped into the spotlight to speak her truth and demonstrate it. What followed was a wonderfully relaxing and invigorating healing session for me and a beautiful and insightful energy medicine session captured on film for posterity.

Now, with this book, Deborah's wisdom extends beyond the screen. Her journey, insights, and unique approach to healing are shared here, offering a roadmap for those ready to listen—to the whispers, the nudges, and, hopefully, before they ever get the hammer.

Beyond Pills and Procedures: What Modern Medicine Misses
by Deborah Cambio

My name is Deborah Cambio, and I facilitate self-healing for those facing physical, emotional, or spiritual challenges. My approach involves identifying core issues and using personalized healing techniques such as chakra balancing, color therapy, sound therapy, energy work, guided visualization, and intuitive guidance. My goal is to help empower individuals to move forward, unlocking their full potential and purpose.

My Spiritual Journey

I was raised Episcopalian and practiced until I was 18 when I realized it no longer resonated with me. Seeking a deeper connection, I embarked on my own spiritual journey. About ten years later, I met a Muslim family, converted to Islam, and spent a decade exploring the faith. While I learned much, I eventually found I resonated more with spirituality in a broader sense. Now, I embrace all religions, believing they share a common goal: seeking truth, love, and connection.

My path to holistic healing evolved over time. I began as a massage therapist, and I started receiving intuitive messages for the clients as I was working on them. This guidance expanded my practice, leading me to integrate various healing modalities. Over the years, I have studied various modalities such as Peruvian shamanic practices, frequency modalities utilizing color, sound, and aromatherapy to help individuals release deep-seated traumas and fears.

The Limitations of Modern Medicine

Modern medicine tends to treat symptoms rather than addressing the whole individual. True healing requires acknowledging the interconnectedness of mind, body, and emotions. The medical system is often fragmented, with specialists working in isolation rather than addressing underlying causes holistically. When doctors incorporate energy-based healing methods, they will better understand the origins of illness and disease.

In my experience, illness often has an emotional root. When emotions are suppressed over time, they can manifest physically as disease. By identifying and releasing these emotional attachments, we create space for true healing. Many healing techniques that were once respected have been dismissed by mainstream medicine, yet they hold great potential for restoring harmony and balance.

Many of my clients seek me out after exhausting conventional medical options, often told there is no explanation for their symptoms. Western medicine frequently overlooks energy imbalances, past traumas, and emotional blockages—factors that must be addressed for true healing to occur.

The Value of Balance, Harmony, and Empowerment

Healing begins with empowerment. One of my most profound realizations is that balance within ourselves—particularly the harmony of our masculine, feminine and inner child aspects—is essential. These aspects exist within everyone and must be in alignment to create wholeness. The masculine aspect represents action, strength, and directing, while the feminine embodies intuition, receptivity, and nurturing. The inner child represents innocence, joy, and freedom. When out of balance, we feel disconnected from our true power. When in harmony, we empower our highest potential and purpose—not as a distant goal, but as something we embody every moment of every day.

Recognizing and Releasing Conditioning

A crucial step in self-healing is recognizing the conditioning we have inherited. Our upbringing, ancestors, and societal expectations often shape our beliefs, habits, and behaviors. Many of these patterns may have served us in childhood, providing a sense of security or survival, but as we step into adulthood, they can become limiting.

These conditioned behaviors manifest in our emotional and physical well-being. Anxiety, chronic illness, and even diseases such as high blood pressure and cancer can often be linked to deeply ingrained beliefs that no longer serve us. Healing requires us to examine where we feel stuck and what no longer serves our conditioned selves, and then consciously choose to recondition our minds and bodies toward balance and health.

What You Most Need to Know About Yourself

From the moment we are born as pure, sovereign beings, we can be conditioned and imprinted out of our empowered state of being. We hold immense power within us—the power to heal, transform, and reclaim our authentic selves.

We are constantly being influenced and conditioned, which can either support or hinder our well-being. When we align with our authentic selves, we remain in a state of ease. However, when we disconnect from that truth, we fall into states of *dis-ease* that manifest in emotional and physical imbalances.

Holding onto unresolved emotions over time can embed them within our physical body, creating illness. When we live in balance and harmony, we enter a state of wholeness, and wholeness empowers us to live fully and freely.

To shift from a state of dis-ease to one of ease, it is essential to identify and address the root cause of our disempowered experiences. Through guided visualization and self-reflection, we can reconnect with the parts of ourselves that became trapped in emotional wounds. Observing, understand, embracing, and releasing these aspects of our being allows us to reclaim our power and return to a state of wholeness.

True empowerment comes from within. When we reach our full potential, we realize that healing is not just about fixing what is broken but about remembering who we truly are.

My Healing Process

One of my clients, a 42-year-old woman, has been caught in a cycle of chronic illness since she was five years old. Her symptoms began with headaches and unexplained fainting spells, which went untreated until she reached the age of 17, when the doctors finally prescribed pharmaceuticals. Over time, she became heavily reliant on the medication without ever identifying the root cause of her condition. In our sessions, we discovered that as an infant she was raised in an environment in which she did not feel safe. This triggered the illness, reinforcing my understanding that *dis-ease* often stems from deeper energetic imbalances that modern medicine does not fully address.

I have been helping her reconnect with her body's natural rhythm using frequency therapy, including sound and color. A key realization in our work together has been the concept of coherence—coming back to the center, to the mark of balance, rather than living in a constant state of *dis-ease*.

I introduced her to the idea that healing is about returning to ease, to a state of neutrality where the body is not in perpetual fight-or-flight mode. She has also been conditioned to believe that medication is the only answer, so our work has been about gently reconditioning her beliefs to explore a more natural, intuitive path to healing.

Because she has been taking medication for decades, this is a delicate process. I emphasize gradual shifts rather than sudden changes, helping her regain trust in her own body. While she initially expressed a desire to stop all medications at once, I advised patience, reminding her that true healing is a journey, not an instant fix. Our sessions are helping her release fear, listen to her body, and step into a more empowered state of well-being.

When working with clients, I tune into their energy, my guides, and theirs. Through intuitive direction, I assess their chakras to identify imbalances. Each session begins with a discussion of their life experiences, which helps me understand how their body, minds, and emotions interact. My role is not to "fix" but to facilitate self-healing, guiding individuals to recognize the patterns and shifts they need to make.

The chakras are seven main energy centers along the spine, each corresponding to a color and element:

- Root Chakra (Red, Earth): This chakra governs survival instincts and grounding. It is concerned with the basic needs such as food, shelter, sleep, and self-preservation. When balanced, we feel grounded, secure, and connected to the earth. When imbalanced, we can feel anxious, insecure, and fearful, with a lack of focus.

- Sacral Chakra (Orange, Water): The sacral chakra influences our emotions, relationships, and creativity. It is linked to the kidneys and governs emotional well-being. When balanced, we feel easy-going and enjoy healthy relationships. When imbalanced, we feel tension, inner conflict, have difficulty expressing emotions, and feel unstable.

- Solar Plexus Chakra (Yellow, Fire): Associated with personal power, confidence, and digestion. Blockages in this chakra often manifest as anxiety, restlessness, and may experience digestive issues or low self-esteem. When balanced, we feel calm, confident, and empowered.

- Heart Chakra (Green, Air): As we might expect, the heart chakra governs love, compassion, and relationships. Grief and heartbreak can deeply affect this chakra. When balanced, we find it easy to forgive, accept, and practice kindness. When unbalanced, we feel jealous, lonely, resentful and suspicious.
- Throat Chakra (Blue, Space): The throat chakra is related to communication and self-expression. A blocked throat chakra can lead to difficulty speaking one's truth. When unbalanced we lack clarity, suppress our emotions, and have difficulty communicating. When balanced, we feel clear, balanced, and expressive.
- Third Eye Chakra (Indigo, Light): Our third eye chakra influences intuition, perception, and inner wisdom. It helps us see beyond the physical and is often associated with psychic vision. When unbalanced we feel confused, forgetful, and disconnected from our intuition.
- Crown Chakra (Violet, Divine Connection): The crown chakra connects to spirituality, consciousness, and universal wisdom. When disconnected we feel listless, depressed, dissatisfied, and anxious.

Every healing session is unique. Depending on a client's needs, I may use shamanic journeying, guided visualizations, crystal therapy, sound healing, or bodywork. My role is to help individuals turn inward, trust their intuition, and reconnect with their authentic selves. By working on a soul level, we can remove obstacles that have persisted for years—or even lifetimes.

The Future of Healing

Healing is a journey of self-discovery. My vision for the future of medicine is that we embrace a system where people take charge of their health and become sufficiently in touch with their bodies to recognize imbalances early. By adopting a holistic approach and integrating complementary methods with conventional medicine, we can achieve balance, harmony, and a deeper connection with ourselves and the world. The more we understand that healing extends beyond the physical—into the emotional, energetic, and spiritual—the more we unlock our true potential.

DEBORAH CAMBIO is a highly respected teacher, spiritual director, massage therapist, and life coach. For over 30 years, Deborah has worked with clients to encourage, empower, and inspire them to come into a fuller realization of their abilities, potential, and purpose. Through her work, Deborah seeks to open her clients to greater self-realization, harmony, balance, and spiritual well-being.

Among her varied practices, Deborah is a massage therapist with certifications in polarity, reiki, aromatherapy, and other healing modalities. She also holds certifications in the FourWinds Program of Peruvian Shamanic Healing Practices, Applied Psychology, and Intuitive Therapeutics.

Deborah's approach as a facilitator is to show what is blocking you from living your highest potential and purpose by helping to release old patterns, beliefs, emotions, and conditioned behaviors that no longer serve. Deborah shares her intuitive perception from a place of unconditional love, non-judgment, and genuine compassion. Her goal is to help others gain awareness and insight to empower themselves, overcome fear, and move more wholly into love.

https://yourempoweredself.org

Gail's Conscious Living Challenge:
Reclaim Your Healing Power

For too long, many of us have been told that our bodies are broken—that they're turning against us, and that the best we can do is manage the decline. Especially with complex, misunderstood conditions like autoimmune disorders or Lyme disease, conventional medicine often fails to offer real answers. And doctors too frequently blame us when they don't know how to help us: it must be your fault.

That narrative is deeply disempowering. And it's time we rewrite it.

What if the body isn't attacking itself at all? What if, instead, it's sounding an alarm—calling our attention to an imbalance, a toxin, a hidden infection, or an unprocessed emotion with nowhere else to go?

As Bruce Lipton states, it's not our genetics but rather our epigenetics—shaped by our lifestyles and emotional processing—that have a more significant impact on us than the genetics of our physical bodies.

We are entering a new era of healing—one rooted in self-discovery, not just prescriptions. As Deborah reminds us, there is no one-size-fits-all solution. Every healing journey is deeply personal, and every healing session should honor the individual's uniqueness and intention.

Medical professionals can be valuable allies but are no longer the sole authority. They are part of the team—not the director. You are the one in the center of your own healing circle.

To truly heal, we must treat the body as a whole system—mind, body, and spirit working together in harmony. This holistic perspective is not a luxury, but rather a necessity for profound, lasting transformation.

Your challenge is to take back the reins and become curious, intuitive, and proactive about your well-being. Start seeing yourself as the leader of your healing journey, and trust that your body possesses wisdom. Healing is possible; it begins when you choose to listen to yourself.

IT'S TIME

Start with this:

- **Question the blame.** If you've been told your body is the problem, pause. What if it's simply communicating something deeper?
- **Embrace individualized healing.** There is no universal path. What works for one person may not work for you—and that's not failure; it's guidance.
- **Set clear intentions.** Just as every healing session is unique, your intention matters. What are you truly seeking in your healing?
- **Explore root causes.** From hidden viral loads to repressed emotional trauma, allow yourself to investigate the real origins beneath your symptoms.
- **Understand your energy body.** From the basic seven to the expanded twelve, the chakras hold keys to emotional and physical imbalances. Learn to read them.
- **Build your healing team, but lead the journey.** Doctors, specialists, and practitioners are there to support you—but you are the director. You set the intention and make the decisions, as you know your body best. You are the guide who steers the journey. Don't hesitate to include holistic therapists and various modalities to support your healing process.
- **Treat yourself as a whole being.** True healing addresses mind, body, and spirit together—not in isolation.
- **Trust your inner healer.** Learn the signals of your body. Follow the subtle nudges. You already have what you need to begin.

9

Introducing Suzy Miller

IN JANUARY 2019, in a conversation with Sandie Sedgbeer, Suzy Miller shared some information she had received telepathically from the Collective Consciousnes of the Children. They told Suzy that they were looking to find a pod that was going to help them integrate. True to her role as a connector, Sandie immediately picked up the phone to bring Suzy and me together. We connected, we cried, and two days later Suzy was on a plane to Denver to check out the Harmonic Egg®. She wanted to know if it was the "pod" the children were asking for. After experiencing the Egg, Suzy said, "the kids came in and said that the Egg was indeed what they had been looking for, and that it would be a good support for them."

Afterward, she confirmed what we all intuitively knew: the Harmonic Egg® holds transformative potential, and she has since shared countless visions with me over the years. Through these shared experiences, Suzy and I have become not only close friends but also colleagues, offering each other support in our respective journeys.

We've been interviewed together on podcasts, with Suzy interviewing me and vice versa. These conversations delve deeper into our story, and I invite you to seek them out online for further exploration.

Suzy's contributions, particularly regarding love and the autistic community, are invaluable. She is helping us understand a vital aspect of humanity's future. I felt bringing her into this film to share her wisdom was important.

Lessons in Love
by Suzy Miller, M.Ed.

Looking back on 1999, the last year of the final decade of the 20th Century, it was easy to believe that humanity was heading into a new golden era. Driven by the rapid rise of dot-com empires, the entire world was basking in the glow of our newfound interconnectivity with its promise of near-instant everything. Futurists and industry experts confidently claimed that technology would change our world drastically.

If anyone had predicted back then that within just one year, I would have swapped my decade-long career as a Pediatric Speech-Language Pathologist with a thriving private practice for an unknown, untested, and financially unstable new "job" working with and being guided by a "freaky" little four-year-old, barely verbal autistic boy who had recruited me to "put his light body back into his physical body," I would have called them crazy.

But that's precisely what happened. And for a while, I wondered if it was me who was crazy. Though I didn't know the right words for it then, I had become a telepathic communicator and integration specialist, trained by that little boy, Riley, to support children like him, who were beginning to arrive on the planet in droves.

At the time, I did not understand what Riley was talking about or if I had the capacity to do what he was asking. But I did know in every fiber of my being that my primary focus from that moment on was to help Riley—and ultimately many thousands of children like him—integrate their light bodies with their physical body experience.

Step-by-step over the following year, Riley took me through a process that included telepathically communicating with me during our therapy sessions and confirming what was received, via writing, visiting me in my dreams, and bi-locating to my house. He told me what I needed to do to integrate his light body with his physical body, and moment by moment, week by week, he began to show up more fully in this world. And as he did, my life began to change, too.

When I first met Riley, my husband was building an office on our property where I could see my speech pathology clients. It never got used for that purpose. When people asked what I was doing, I would explain some of what I was experiencing with this little boy. Word got out, and soon, people in my community were bringing their children to me in droves. By the time the year ended, my pediatric speech pathologist practice had transformed into a full-time healing practice.

However, it wasn't entirely unproblematic. When a pediatric speech-language pathologist with a strong focus on science and education suddenly starts talking about light bodies, integration, and communicating telepathically with children telling you how to facilitate their ability to communicate, it doesn't go down very well with one's colleagues. I had to deal with a lot of ridicule. People would look at me and say, "What are you talking about?" Or "I don't believe that is possible." But I was so caught up in working with Riley and learning directly from him that I didn't care. He was showing me that he and I were both so much more than were previously thought to be possible and I was enthralled by this awareness and the process he was guiding me through.

Riley is now in his late 20s. If you saw him today, you might say he looks autistic. The most notable change, however, is that he is now fully verbal and communicating. Equally significant is how this journey transformed his parents, both of whom experienced profound personal growth. His mother now works with children on the spectrum.

You can read more about my early years with Riley and other children on the spectrum in my book, *Awesomism: A New Way to Understand the Diagnosis of Autism*. After publishing it in 2008, parents worldwide reached out, saying they'd had telepathic and healing experiences with their children but had never found the words to express them.

What I want to share with you now are the extraordinary events that unfolded later—when the collective consciousness of these children began to reveal itself to me. Think of this as a collective voice that I heard telepathically that held all the information that was common to souls who were born into this world and who would later be diagnosed with autism. They told me who they truly are, why they couldn't fully be here yet, what they need us to understand, and most importantly, why they are here.

After working with Riley for a while, the number of individual children diagnosed with autism that I worked with continued to increase. Over time, their telepathic messages became one growing voice. And as the years passed, the voices with that collective consciousness also included those of individuals I had never personally seen but were clearly part of the autism community. It was like hearing a crowd of people speaking all at once. I would ask them questions about various things and they would give me information to help other children integrate more readily. They would provide specific instructions like, "This is what you need to tell our parents so that they can become aware that we are "in here" and how to be of real support." And they guided and trained me in advanced energetic processes that would help them.

From the very start, the children told me they hadn't arrived with autism—they came with Awesomism, which they defined as a higher state of consciousness trying to interface with the density of conditioned human consciousness. They asked for my help in shifting the perception of autism through this word.

The word "Awesomism" plays a crucial role in the story of autism because so many people view this population as broken, dysregulated, or in need of fixing. In reality, they don't need to be fixed; they need understanding, love, compassion, and awareness. The shift they wanted wasn't just about language; it was about transforming how they are perceived and what they, as souls, have come to do for humanity. Once that perception changes, it opens the door for people to see them through a completely new lens that recognizes their true gifts and potential.

Next, they and those who read *Awesomsim* asked me to develop the "Awesomism Practitioner" process to bring together parents and professionals from various backgrounds to share and build on their collective knowledge, telepathic skills, and ability to see these children for who they really are. I created and led the practitioner training, personally guiding around 300 individuals to date across 15 countries.

Meantime, the children continued to give me information about vaccines and other environmental toxins and the education system. They said all the old, outdated systems and ways of being in the world would start breaking down, and they were here to help with that. And they predicted many other things that have since come to pass. One of these was that I would work on an important project with a scientist to help advance the awareness of intention as it relates to supporting the integration of those on the spectrum.

In 2011, I was introduced to the late Dr. William Tiller, Stanford Emeritus Professor of Materials Science. A Fellow of the American

Academy for the Advancement of Science and the author of four books and hundreds of peer-reviewed papers on intention and consciousness, Dr. Tiller had spent over four decades avocationally pursuing serious experimental and theoretical study in the field of psychoenergetics with a special focus on the power of coherent intention to change physical reality. A featured physicist in the popular movie, *What the Bleep Do We Know?* Dr. Tiller had conducted numerous scientific experiments demonstrating the power of coherent intention to create positive change in the physical world.

United by a common focus, Bill and I decided in late 2012 to create and collaborate on the world's first scientifically monitored research study into the power of coherent intention to manifest change in the physical domain. The Autism Intention Experiment Research Program was unique in that the physical domain of rigorous science, educational and medical awareness and considerations, the spiritual domain of metaphysics, and the connections associated with that realm were interwoven throughout all aspects of the program.

As any parent or educator working with children diagnosed with autism will attest, these children clearly have their attention elsewhere. They seem preoccupied beyond the physical world, focused on something beyond the mind and body. According to the insights they've shared with me, children diagnosed with autism are naturally more comfortable directing their focus toward subtle, often unperceived, realms of human experience. Due to their unique energetic and neurological makeup, they are attuned to aspects of reality that most people do not perceive. In essence, they engage more with the unseen because they cannot be conditioned to believe that the physical world is all there is.

If this assessment is accurate, supporting these children in becoming more present in the physical world requires us to step beyond our own comfort zones—into the subtle domain of spirit. And that is precisely what Tillerian physics and technology facilitate!

Until then, autism and most other "conditions" had been approached through a traditional model rooted in an outdated Copernican theory. This outdated model focused solely on diagnosis and symptom management using standard therapeutic, educational, biochemical, dietary, and pharmaceutical interventions. Because it operated only within the physical and mental domains, it emphasized a limited "window of opportunity"—before age seven—for optimal progress in communication and cognitive function.

However, this approach overlooked a fundamental truth: we are not just body and mind but also spirit.

The Tiller/Miller Integration Model for autism, developed by Bill and me, moves beyond the traditional approach and is based on the following principles:

- A human being is more than just a physical body ("bio-body suit") and mental projections.
- The physical body simply allows us to experience the world through space and time.
- True integration involves incorporating all aspects of the self—physical, emotional, mental, and more subtle realms—into a whole while also recognizing the role of spirit (the unseen domains) in supporting the integration process.
- Improved functioning occurs through holistic *integration* of body, mind, and spirit, without diminishing the unique essence and gifts these individuals bring to humanity.
- In autism, integration happens through an *interactive* experience between parent and child and the unseen factors that positively or negatively bind them together. Every child can integrate in their own way, regardless of age or cognitive ability, provided these unseen factors are acknowledged and made conscious.
- Traditional models can also be valuable if they support the child without harming their body, mind, or spirit. For this population, we must always consider not just what is being done to support them, but the intention with which it is done.

An integration-based approach is essential. Through decades of learning directly from these children, I have come to see this as the future of education and medicine—provided humanity embraces supporting these children without asking them to abandon who they truly are.

With guidance from the Collective Consciousness of the Children, and Bill's expertise in formulating coherent intentions, we created a two-fold intention statement. This statement was designed to condition the physical space to support the children's integration and reduce stress for their parents, tailored to each family's unique needs. The intention was set in love and aligned with each child's soul directive. The results, analyzed by one of Professor Tiller's statistician colleagues, were deemed 'statistically significant.'

My purpose in sharing this is to highlight the groundbreaking conclusion of 45 years of Professor William Tiller's research, combined with over 30 years of telepathic communication with children on the autism spectrum: *both the conscious and the subconscious minds affect matter.*

Simply put, *your mind is your most powerful tool, and your intention is a force like no other.*

The journey toward integration begins with the parents. Initially, many struggle to understand a child who seems so different. But through education, self-awareness, and compassion, these parents start to see their children not as a source of trauma but as teachers—guiding their families to integrate unconscious parts of themselves that have long been buried. In this process, not only do the children grow, but so do the parents, which leads to deeper love, connection, and co-creation within the family unit.

Children diagnosed with autism are the forerunners of what we might call the "new human." They are prototypes, embodying qualities that are part of the future of humanity. These children come with abilities like telepathy, healing, and reading emotions, minds, and even physical states—gifts that we all have the potential to access as we evolve. I see them as the next step in human evolution, a new species.

These children not only know things that we do not yet know but are also far more connected to the concept of unity than most humans have been throughout history. Coming from a place of unified consciousness—what I would call love—they hold the template for wholeness while simultaneously struggling to manifest that expression through their bodies. They understand love, unity, and what truly brings people together instead of what separates us. Think of their souls in unity consciousness and their bodies in separation. This alone creates the dysregulation that we notice in the physical world.

Many parents have shared that they feel their families are falling apart because of these children. However, what's fascinating is that this population constantly invites those around them to look deeper within themselves. They challenge us to unify the parts of ourselves that we've neglected or failed to love and to bring that unity into our relationships with our children and each other.

For over 30 years of working with children diagnosed with autism, I've witnessed their evolution from childhood to adulthood, and their journeys have illuminated a profound shift for those around them and in our collective consciousness. These children, who once seemed misunderstood, are now advocating for themselves in ways we never anticipated—spelling out their messages, expressing their thoughts, and bridging communication gaps in communication that were previously thought impossible.

What has become clear is that supporting the integration of these children is not just a personal journey but a societal one. The children born today are far more integrated than those in the 1980s when autism first began to emerge on a larger scale. This shift is largely due to the lessons learned from the children and those working alongside them. Through these years of observation and collaboration, interfacing these children, as they should be, within society has begun to become smoother. Although they still embody a higher frequency—often feeling almost like they're from another species—the path to integration is now far more accessible.

What we are witnessing is nothing short of revolutionary. These children are not just challenging the way we view autism but are reshaping our understanding of human potential itself. With their heightened intuitive, telepathic, and multidimensional abilities—skills available to all of us as we evolve as a human species—they are urging us to expand the boundaries of what we consider possible. While their behaviors may seem challenging, they are not signs of dysfunction; they are expressions of the extraordinary vibrational frequency they bring into the world. These children may struggle to fully embody their high-frequency energy in a world not yet ready for it, but their very presence is already igniting change, shifting science, education, medicine, technology, and even how we connect with each other.

The rise in autism diagnoses—from 1 in 10,000 children in the 1980s to 1 in 43 today—is not simply due to advancements in diagnostic tools or the rapid increase of vaccines. Although both play a role, as there are many contributing factors, to indicate that anything is the full reason is to negate who these children actually are. They are here for a reason. They bring a frequency of love and unity, pushing humanity toward a greater sense of collective evolution. In fact, when I asked these children why they've incarnated now, their answer was clear: they were called by humanity's collective need for transformation. We asked for them and their souls heard that call. They arrived to help us evolve.

There are no coincidences here. It is not a coincidence that we are watching all the old structures and systems fall apart since they began to arrive *en masse*.

And it is not a coincidence that the statistics are now more evenly split between male and female children.

The changes these children catalyze are part of a more significant shift unfolding in our world. As we face growing societal division, they remind us that the solution lies in unity, love, and understanding, not divisiveness. They invite us to integrate more fully with ourselves and each other and to evolve alongside them, to look within and see where we are divided from ourselves and from those around us. Do we live our lives from a place of seeking to unify? Do we make connections or divisions? Do we buy into the divisiveness projected daily on the evening news? Or do we pay attention to how we are all interconnected?

In short, these children are not anomalies—they are the forerunners of a new human consciousness. Their arrival marks the beginning of a profound shift toward love, unity, and higher-frequency living, and they are here to help us evolve if we are ready to listen and learn.

As mentioned earlier, intention is transformative, especially when paired with love and compassion. From the first child who intended to integrate his light body with his physical body to the children I work with today who have deep intentions to verbally or otherwise communicate—I've seen firsthand how intention, fueled by love, can achieve the seemingly impossible.

When you set a clear intention with love and invite others to join you in that intention, there is nothing that cannot be accomplished. The children diagnosed with autism have gifted me with some of the most extraordinary experiences, and I believe their lessons can change the world.

One of the most often-repeated statements I've heard from every child I've interacted with over the years, and the collective consciousness of children, is that they "could not fully land here on planet Earth until here was the frequency of love."

The children are landing. The more we collectively choose love, the more we will see firsthand evidence of this.

It's time to start choosing love.

~

SUZY MILLER M. Ed. has been CEO and Founder of Blue Star Education and Research, LLC since 1999. Her company is dedicated to supporting the integration of children diagnosed with autism, by expanding parents' understanding of what their children's behaviors are expressing about their innate capacities; the by-product of which is greater connection, communication and co-creation between parent and child. A former pediatric speech-language pathologist with a master's degree in education, Suzy's finely honed abilities to read energy and see and communicate with the unseen have given birth to three pioneering and perception-shifting programs: The Autism Integration Series, The Awesomism Practitioner Process and the New World Portal Community.

www.suzymiller.com

Gail's Conscious Living Challenge:
Choose Love, Engage the Moment, And Let It Flow

Suzy has changed my life in more ways than I can count. I'm so grateful for her presence, her teachings, and how she's helped me open to new dimensions of healing. Truly—and yes, pun intended—there are no words.

I began learning nonverbal communication when I got my horse, Holly, in 2012. I didn't realize it then, but Holly was introducing me to a deeper connection—one that would eventually lead me to the autistic community.

At the time, I had heard stories of healers struggling with autistic children—stories of outbursts, even violence, that made me hesitant and a little afraid. When I met Suzy and shared how I felt, she assured me: "They will never be violent with you. because you're coming from love."

She explained that adverse reactions often stem from inauthentic energy—when someone isn't fully present or aligned, it creates discomfort. That insight shifted everything for me. People—*any* people—aren't "bad." But they *do* pick up on energy. And when that energy doesn't feel genuine or safe, there's always a reaction. Sometimes it's confusion. Sometimes it's resistance. But it's never random.

What I learned from Suzy is the power of compassion—the importance of showing up with genuine love, patience, and authenticity, without expecting perfection or performance in return. That realization gave me the courage to engage from the heart, without fear.

She helped me feel safe—not just in connecting with people on the spectrum, but in trusting the energy of love itself. It's more than a full-time job—it's a lifestyle. There isn't a waking hour I'm not thinking about how to support others on their healing journey, while still holding balance in my own life.

Like so many true healers, Suzy has faced burnout and challenges. We all have. To help others heal, we must be nourished, centered, and whole ourselves. I cherish the small, meaningful moments of connection. Not long ago, I was at the grocery store when a young girl came up to me and told me she loved my shirt. Her mother rushed over, trying to pull her away—likely used to people reacting with discomfort. But I welcomed the moment. I engaged with the girl for a few minutes, and it was lovely. I could feel the mother's appreciation—that someone saw her child not as a disruption, but as a gift.

So here's my final challenge to you:

Engage when you're approached. Whether it's a child or adult on the spectrum, a stranger, or someone different from you—engage. Let the interaction be what it is.

Don't judge the experience. Step beyond expectations and into the subtle realm of energy. As Suzy says, this is the *domain of spirit*.

Let it flow. Release the need to control what "should" happen. When we move without expectation, we invite grace.

Choose love and kindness first. These are not soft emotions—they are the strongest forces we have for healing and connection.

Notice how you feel afterward. Your heart may feel fuller. Your energy lighter. You may remember what it feels like to truly walk this Earth together.

When we lead with love, we create safety for others.

When we engage from authenticity, we are received.

And when we allow the dance of energies to unfold without control... we discover just how much beauty we've been missing.

EPILOGUE

It's Time

In a world on the verge of transformation, *It's Time* is more than just a statement—it's a call to the soul. It urges us to remember our true selves beneath the conditioning, chaos, and cultural noise. It calls us to reclaim the extraordinary power that lies dormant within each of us. Because if nothing else has become clear through the pages of this book and film, it is this: we are not broken—we are becoming.

For centuries, we've been taught to look outward for answers—toward doctors, experts, institutions, and systems. We've been conditioned to seek security, validation, and authority outside of ourselves. But that time is ending. The veil is lifting. We are awakening to the truth that has always been within reach: that healing, wellness, fulfillment, and connection are not bestowed—they are remembered. They begin not in a pill or a program, but in the moment that we choose to reclaim our sovereignty.

We are frequency beings living in a vibrational universe. The science is catching up with what the mystics have always known. Our thoughts shape our biology. Our emotions affect our cells. Our beliefs create our experiences. Everything is energy—and the state of our energy determines the quality of our lives. When we align with higher frequencies—like love, gratitude, joy, and curiosity—we unlock the body's natural ability to heal, the heart's ability to connect, and the soul's ability to lead.

A critical part of our journey to remembering who we are and who we can evolve to become is to take positive steps to clear away all that we are not... we are not an illness. We are not disease. We are not who we have been conditioned to believe we are. We are conscious beings living on a conscious planet in a conscious universe. Wherever your path to clearing away all that you are not leads you—to the Harmonic Egg, or to some other alternative or complementary healing therapy or modality—remember this:

> You are a vibrational being of light from Source, from God. Everything—and I do mean *everything*—on this planet is energy. How you perceive and react to life events determines what

experiences you attract into your life, including your health. Your reactions impact the frequency of your vibrations. By raising your vibrations, you become more empowered and able to take responsibility for yourself, your health, your life, and your world. What I think, do, and say affects you. What you think, do, and say affects me and everyone around you. When any of us commits ourselves to a path of healing, we heal ourselves, each other, and our world. We cannot get away from that. We are not one individual. We are a collective, and understanding and fully embracing this is where our future lies.

New technologies are coming out daily—well, maybe not *daily*, but close. These are not devices that "heal" you, but technologies that create the right environment for your body to heal itself. They offer us opportunities to relax more deeply, to release trauma at the cellular level, and to reconnect with Source. These technologies won't save us—but they can help us listen more carefully to the wisdom of our own bodies. They can help us trust what we know. As we move through this chaotic era of transformation and beyond, we are being asked to take responsibility for our health, our energy, and our evolution. Be discerning. Some tools will uplift you. Others won't. Choose what resonates.

You are a powerful being. You can manifest anything you desire. You just need to believe and train your mind. Healing ourselves heals others. Living in judgment dims your frequency. Living in love raises it. Don't be afraid of love, even if you don't understand those around you or walk a different path. Offer kindness anyway. Because love changes things. Sometimes, it even changes truth.

Love is the highest vibration. The power of the energy of love is transformative. It lifts you above negativity, chaos, and drama. It strengthens your courage, clarifies your path, connects you to your inner light, and rises up to meet those around you, too. Love is the energy of your divine, authentic self. And the more you choose to align with it—through your thoughts, your words, and your actions—the more you become a living conduit for change.

The stories shared in this book—from the breakthroughs in frequency medicine and emerging energy technologies to the deeply personal awakenings of purpose, love, and the rising consciousness of our newest generations—are a reflection of this greater shift in awareness. They reveal a tapestry of transformation that is already underway, one infant, one child, one person at a time. Each experience, innovation, and act of kindness or courage is a thread in the new paradigm woven through us all. It's time to let go of the limiting stories we've inherited. It's time to question the narratives that keep us small and afraid. It's time to see ourselves—not as victims of circumstance—but as co-creators of a new world.

Here are a few suggestions for how to raise your vibration, elevate your mood, and reconnect to the knowing within you:

Be realistic: Avoid trying to jump from despair to joy all at once. Instead, aim for the next best feeling.

Start Your Day Positively: Engage in uplifting activities such as exercising, spending time in nature, practicing silence, expressing gratitude, and connecting with others.

Surround Yourself with Uplifting People: Trust your intuition when identifying individuals who enhance your mood and energy.

Practice Daily Gratitude: This simple habit can transform feelings of scarcity into a sense of sufficiency and turn fear into appreciation.

Help Others: Assisting someone else is one of the quickest ways to improve your own mood.

Play: Remember that your inner child holds the key to joy, so allow yourself time for fun.

Accept That Progress Isn't Linear: Healing is not always a straightforward process and can vary over time. Embrace the natural ebb and flow of your emotions.

Always Remember That You Have Choice: If you feel yourself dipping into shame, anger, or despair, take one small step upward—one choice toward light. That's how healing happens. That's how we evolve.

The world around us is shifting fast. As the film and this book explore, we are not just witnessing a breakdown—we are being invited into a breakthrough. Penny Kelly said it best: "We can no longer look at change as if we are innocent bystanders caught in the storm." We are the storm—and the solution. If we want a different world, we must become it.

Let's be honest: The old ways aren't working. Hate, greed, division, hierarchy, disconnection—these energies are exhausting and outdated. They are the residue of fear. But fear is not who we are. We are love. We are possibility. We are connection.

So how do we begin creating a new world?
We start by reclaiming what has always been true: that we are powerful, connected, intelligent, and inherently worthy of wholeness.

Let's reimagine what healing looks like—not as sterile buildings filled with fluorescent lights but as spaces of true restoration. Let's dream of frequency-based centers, gardens of peace, music that soothes the soul, and ancient practices integrated with future-facing technologies. Let's envision spaces filled with light, nature, community, and compassion—places where people come not just to recover but to remember who they are.

Let's remember—we're not just talking about personal healing here. This is planetary healing. This is paradigm-shifting transformation. As Dr. Stephen Post and the Unlimited Love Institute have shown, love isn't just a virtue—it's medicine. Compassion, service, and giving literally make us healthier, happier, more fulfilled. When we live from love, we don't just survive—we thrive.

This isn't only about alternative health, energy medicine, or healing trauma. It's about remembering that we are the medicine. Love isn't just a feeling—it's a frequency. And when we embody it—live it, speak it, radiate it—we become powerful forces for change.

Let this book be a mirror to your truth, a guide through the fog of forgetting, and a spark that lights the fire of transformation within you. Let it remind you that your body is wise, your intuition is real, and your journey matters. Let it give you the courage to take your next step—however small—toward living a life aligned with your deepest truth.

It's Time is a reminder, an invitation, and a call to believe in your power, follow your inner knowing, walk the path of love—even when it's hard—and be the change, not just in theory, but in frequency.

And most of all, let it inspire you to stay open. Stay grounded in your heart, even when the world feels heavy. Because the world needs you—not the masked version, not the "fixed" version—but the real, radiant, remembering you.

It's time—to believe in yourself. To trust your path. To choose love, again and again. Because when we heal ourselves, we heal each other. When we do it with love, we raise the frequency of the world. When we remember who we are, we remind others who they are. And when enough of us wake up... everything changes.

It's time.

Appendices

APPENDIX I

10 Steps to Reinventing Our World
by Penny Kelly

Our world needs a boost and some positive energy! It needs a revival of spirit, adventure, and possibility. It needs you and everything that you have to offer. And we need one another. This is something we know deep inside. We can't make it without one another. We can't do life alone. The problem is that we have never been taught to work together unless we're working for a corporation and collecting a paycheck. This won't work if we want to change our society. We have to work together because we want to create something new.

The steps to re-inventing our world are not rocket science, but they do require time, energy, commitment, and the creative efforts of everyone. If we are going to build a new world, we humans must work together taking the steps, one by one, that will build a bridge to a New Earth.

1. First, we must look around and assess where we are at in our lives, what is working or not working.

2. Next, we must begin conversations about our situation. These conversations must be open and free, honest and clear, and we must learn to listen deeply to one another as we share what is working for us personally, as well as what we would like to see in our future.

3. A careful assessment should be made of what is worth keeping and what can be revised or updated to work well. What is not beneficial should be left behind. This assessment should include extensive lists of resources—including people, skills, plants, animals, and machinery—all of which should be written down.

4. Goals, principles, and processes that will lead to the world we want to live in must be decided and set in place. These goals should also be written as part of an initial plan, yet be regularly reviewed and revised as experience changes us and our ideas.

5. Then, as an interim step, we must reconnect to Mother Nature in order to re-establish a base level of security to steady us while we begin the necessary changes that can sometimes cause us to feel vulnerable and unsettled.

6. Transition structures are next and must be created to address gaps, uneven distribution, poverty, and other shortcomings we identified in our initial assessment of what is working and not working.

7. Once we get moving in the right direction, leadership must be constantly appraised and re-evaluated to make sure we are listening to the right people. There should be a concerted effort to develop a variety of leaders in order to avoid the emergence of strongmen that try to take over and run everything.

8. There must be an ongoing process of rethink, reorganize, rebuild, and review the transition structures because these structures will only be appropriate for a time. We must be willing to revise and revise again until stability, long-term structures, and homeostasis are achieved.

9. Once homeostasis has been reached, we can focus on further development of ourselves and our consciousness in order to further develop our systems, institutions, and technologies. Trying to push further development of systems, institutions and technologies before we are ready would result in premature decisions and poor outcomes. Failing to take time out periodically to focus on further development of consciousness would result in an inability for the New Earth to blossom fully.

10. We will know we are succeeding when we see peace, experience security, and have lives that are enhanced by technology instead of threatened by it. We will have good health and the high creativity of an awakened consciousness, and we will discover joy in the simplicity of The Everyday.

APPENDIX II

A Meditation for Mother Earth
Renewing Your Connection to Mother Earth
A Meditation with Penny Kelly

This is a meditation for Mother Earth. You need a renewed connection to Her, and She needs to know you care, that you are listening, that you have more to offer this world than your fear, irritation, or hurt.

Go outside and sit on the ground. Not in a chair. Put your butt on the ground. If it is difficult for you to sit up straight, be aware of how much core strength you have lost and make a mental note to do something about that later. For the moment, however, put your hands in the grass, the sand, the soil, or whatever you're sitting on. Your hands will help prop you up for this brief meditation. If you live in an apartment in a big city, imagine you are leaving the body and going to a local park or the beach to sit on the ground.

Once your hands are on the ground, imagine that you can feel the entire earth in the palm of your hands as if you had a giant beach ball glued to your palms. It would be like sitting on a big beach ball! Wiggle your thumbs and fingers to get Mother Earth's attention and then simply say hello to her. Tell her you love her and that you would like to reconnect with her. Then stop. Ask yourself what that reconnection might consist of. Would it be that you send her a happy thought or two every day? Might it be a promise to check in with her once a week and just ask what she needs? Would it be an effort to notice the beauty she displays from season to season, or a deep gratitude for the way the entire system works together to support and nurture life of so many kinds? Whatever it is, tell her what your reconnection would be so she knows what it would look like and will recognize both it and you. Then, invite her to send messages to you. Tell her you promise to pay attention to her messages. And then just sit quietly with her for a moment the way you might sit with a friend or a lover.

As you sit there, become aware of what you can hear. Do you hear only the sounds of humans and their tools and toys? If so, listen more deeply for the sounds of flying things like bees and bugs. Listen for the sound of birds talking to one another across the distances. Be aware that they are letting one another know what is going on in their territory. Listen for the sound of the wind and breezes moving. Listen for the whisper of leaves as they move about in their constant effort to position and re-position themselves like little, green solar panels trying to catch the most sunlight.

Listen for the rustling in the bushes or among the trees for squirrels or chipmunks going about their daily search for food and water and be grateful for the many systems we have set up to make our lives easier. If you live near moving water, listen for the voice of the creek or the pounding of the ocean and thank it for reminding you that you are mostly water and need to keep yourself moving.

Then lay back and put your head on Mother Earth. Yes, you may have to wash your hair later or at least brush it to get the bits of nature out of it. As you lay there, become aware of your entire body. Do you feel things landing on you or bugs crawling on you? Are you afraid they will bite you? If this frightens you, become aware of how fearful you have become and how distant you are from the community of life on Mother Earth. Remind yourself and the things crawling on you that you are more than just some kind of landing post or something to pick at and eat. If this seems awkward or they do not stop, ask yourself, how is it you have lost your ability to communicate with all things and ask them to not bite or harm you? How many other things are you afraid of? When was the last time you talked to the sun or the butterfly fluttering through your yard? What is your relationship with Mr. Wind or Ms. Water? Do you have relationships with these elements? What do you need to do in order to get back into the community of life?

APPENDIX II

Everything is alive and has some form of consciousness. It may not look or sound like human consciousness, but it is aware of its form and seeks to build itself up into something better. Ask yourself: What are you seeking?

Is it something temporary or something more long-term?

Is what you seek frilly or shallow… Or is it deeply useful and leads to your greater wisdom, power, and grace?

Are you aware that you have emerged from the complex of energies, minerals, and forms of life that are common to Mother Earth?

Think about that for a moment… then celebrate your own life!

Now sit up and look around you. See the world as it truly is. Become aware that Mother Earth requires presence from her people, and ask yourself, *are you present?*

Then thank the entire community of life that you are part of.

Give yourself permission to feel joy. And now get up and go about your day, keeping a touch of that joy and a sense of belonging with you.

Have a wonderful day!

You can listen to a recording of this meditation using the link and/or QR code below.

https://www.youtube.com/watch?v=VNF_e4_3Zv0

APPENDIX III

Techniques for Bio-hacking Anxiety
by Dr. Synthia Andrews

Change, especially chaotic change, can be overwhelming and spark anxiety. It's easy to lose sight of inner resources and resiliency. Here are two quick ways to circumvent anxiety using principles of neuroplasticity and energy balancing; one to be done privately, and one that can be used when feeling anxious in the midst of activity. The techniques use three tools: visualization, affirmation, and physical cues. Try them as written, then change them to best fit you.

TECHNIQUE NUMBER ONE: Use when you are in a quiet space and will not be disturbed. Time for completion is 3-5 minutes.

1. **Physical Cue: Lateral Eye Movements**
   This practice decouples the amygdala (emotional center of the brain) from the cerebral cortex (thinking center), reducing emotional charge and re-establishing awareness of your center.

   - Allow fear or anxiety to be as big as it wants to be. No need to repress or change it.
   - Raise your arms to shoulder height and curl your fists with thumbs up.
   - Separate your arms to the point you can easily see both thumbs in your peripheral vision while looking straight ahead.
   - Keep your face pointed straight ahead and, moving your eyes only, lookback and forth from thumb to thumb.

2. **Affirmation: Self-talk instructs the neurocircuitry of the brain.**
   The way we talk to ourselves can increase catastrophic thinking and create interference in our frequency or it can help us center and

ground, improving our coherence and creating new neurocircuitry. Create affirmations that are spoken in present-time and are believable. Also, speak the affirmation in third person and use your name as if someone else is talking to you. This encourages your brain to respond and shift. Here are some examples:

- Right here, right now, you have everything you need. You are safe.
- You can do this; you are strong, confident, and courageous.
- Every problem has a solution.
- Inside, you have everything you need.
- You are not alone. Help is always available.
- Anxiety is a feeling created in your past. It has no power in the present.

3. **Visualization: Visualization is a powerful tool to create new neuropathways.**
Visualization is used by athletes, public speakers, CEOs and everyone who wants to improve their ability to be clear, responsive, grounded, and centered.

- Picture yourself facing the situation causing you anxiety while behaving according to the affirmation you're using.
- If every problem has a solution, imagine yourself solving the problem. See yourself addressing the problem with strength, courage, and confidence.
- The more clearly you can see yourself living the affirmation, the more powerful it will be.
- If you can't imagine it, the affirmation isn't believable to you. Reframe it until you have a statement that reflects what you need and is easy for you to imagine yourself doing.

4. **Putting it all together:**
   - Spend 30 to 60 seconds doing lateral eye movements.
   - Stop the lateral movements, close your eyes, speak your affirmation.

- While repeating your affirmation, visualize yourself successfully doing it.
- Repeat at least 3 times.
- Do as many times in a day as you can. Repetition improves neuroplasticity.

TECHNIQUE NUMBER TWO: Use for quick centering and grounding when faced with something overwhelming.

1. **Physical cue:** this arrangement de-activates your kidney meridian, the meridian that generates fear, sending the energy into Earth to establish grounding.
   - Place your left hand over your sternum (chest bone). There is a hollow on either side of the sternum directly under the collarbone. Press your middle finger into the right hollow, and your thumb into the left hollow. These acupoints are the last point on the Kidney meridian, Kidney 27.
   - Place your right hand on your lower abdomen, below your belly button and above your pubic bone. This is your Tan Dien and is centering as well as grounding. In addition, it slows the rise of energy along the kidney meridian.
   - Put your attention on your feet, noticing the ground. Where your mind goes, energy follows.
   - It's perfectly fine to switch hands in the two positions—do what feels natural.

2. Use an affirmation as in technique 1.

3. Visualize acting according to the affirmation.

4. If your attention is needed for action and you can't do steps 2 and 3, no problem. Just keep your hands in the position of the physical cue and maintain awareness of your feet as much as possible.

5. If you need your hands, return to the position whenever you can, or visualize holding the position.

6. It sounds silly, but the hand positions are deeply soothing as the energy charge in the kidney meridian is reduced. The Tan Dien helps centering, and grounding is established through the feet.

APPENDIX IV

A Daily Guide for Living in Love

by Steven A. Ross, Ph.D.

I created my own philosophical regime embodying a beautiful heart, an open mind and a humble spirit. You live this with love, in love and through love. Please elaborate upon a daily living of these precepts.

A beautiful heart, an open mind, and a humble spirit, all animated by love. This is a sacred path; a living philosophy that can truly transform the way one moves through the world. Here is how you embody this as a daily rhythm, a way of being:

1. **A Beautiful Heart.**
   Daily Living Practice: A beautiful heart is felt, not just seen. It radiates kindness, empathy, and compassion, even in the smallest of gestures.

   - **Begin each day with stillness.** Before the world rushes in, place your hand over your heart and breathe in gratitude—for breath, for being, for the mystery of life.
   - **Practice micro-moments of compassion.** A sincere smile, a kind word, and attentiveness are the daily expressions of a beautiful heart.
   - **Refuse resentment.** If someone hurts or frustrates you, choose understanding over reaction. Ask, "What might they be going through?" Transform judgment into empathy.
   - **Engage in beauty.** Surround yourself with music, nature, poetry, and art that softens the soul and inspires tenderness.

2. **An Open Mind**
   Daily Living Practice: An open mind is a fertile ground—curious, willing, and non-defensive. It is the mind of the eternal student, always learning.

- **Question with wonder.** Not to dismantle, but to deepen. Ask: "What else might be true?" or "What can I learn from this?"
- **Listen more than you speak.** Especially to those who think differently. Listening is a radical act of openness.
- **Let go of needing to be right.** Truth is vast and multi-faceted. Be willing to shed old beliefs when a higher truth emerges.
- **Explore something new.** Read from a different tradition. Walk a new path. Try unfamiliar food. Let openness become a daily delight.

3. **A Humble Spirit**
   Daily Living Practice: A humble spirit walks lightly. It does not shrink, nor does it boast. It recognizes the sacred in all and bows often—to others, to life, to mystery.

   - **Start the day with reverence.** Speak aloud or silently: "Guide me today. Let me serve something greater than myself."
   - **Admit when you don't know.** There is power in saying, "I'm still learning." Wisdom begins in that soft space.
   - **Serve quietly.** Do things without needing recognition. Let your actions be the prayer.
   - **See the divine in all.** Whether in a child, a stranger, or someone difficult—greet them inwardly: "Namaste. The Light in me sees the Light in you."

All in Love, With Love, Through Love

Daily Living Practice:

- **Love as Presence:** Be *with* what is, without trying to fix, control, or escape. Love is the space in which transformation occurs.
- **Love as Action:** Let love guide choices—not ego, fear, or ambition. Ask often: "What would Love do here?"
- **Love as Essence:** Remember you *are* love—not separate from it. Return to this truth when the mind wanders.

A Sample Day in This Living Philosophy:

- **Morning:** Wake in silence. Light a candle. Place hand on heart. Whisper gratitude. Breathe in love.
- **Midday:** Smile at strangers. Listen deeply. Take nothing personally. Choose kindness over control.
- **Evening:** Reflect gently. What did you learn today? Where did you love well? Where can you soften tomorrow?

This path is both sacred and simple. Not always easy, but always worth it. And in walking it, you become a living poem—a soft light, a sacred presence, a reminder that love *is* the way.

A Beautiful Heart, An Open Mind, A Humble Spirit

— A Daily Poem for Living in Love
In morning hush, before the sun,
Place your hand where life has begun.
Let gratitude rise, not needing a name,
For breath, for being, for love's quiet flame.

A Beautiful Heart.
Give kindness freely, like petals on breeze,
Offer your presence, the soul's gentle ease.
Smile as prayer, and let anger depart—
Each moment's a canvas to paint with your heart.
See through the eyes of a soul awake,.
Forgive the wound, for compassion's sake.
Speak with warmth that melts the frost—
To hold a grudge is too great a cost.

An Open Mind.
Let wonder guide you more than belief,
Each thought a river, each question a leaf.
Say not "I know," but "I'm here to see"—
Truth wears many robes, flows endlessly.
Listen like earth absorbs the rain,

Hold no need to conquer or explain.
Let curiosity dance like a child,
Barefoot in thought, tender and wild.

A Humble Spirit.

Bow to the sky, to the stone, to the sea,
To the mystery humming in all you see.
Not less than the stars, yet no higher than grass,
Humility shines like dew on glass.
Speak when moved, be still when not,
Serve without seeking to be forgot.
Let the sacred rise in your simplest act—
The way you love is your soul's contract.

In Love, With Love, Through Love.

Let love be breath, not just a word,
The silence beneath all that is heard.
Let love be the lens, the path, the fire—
Not clung to, but lived through, ever higher.
So walk, not to prove but to bless,
Leave behind noise, carry gentleness.
And when the night returns once more,
Lay down in peace, love at your core.

APPENDIX V

Breathing and Toning for Well-being
by Ani Williams

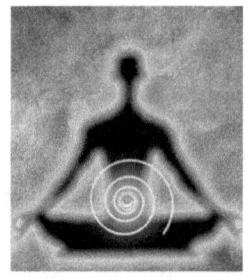

Breathing, chanting, and toning from the belly is a powerful way to shift our state of being and voice quality. I originally learned to focus the breath and energy from the hara (dantian) naval center during classes in Aikido, and later I discovered a similar belly centered breathing during an extended course in Sanskrit traditional chanting. Expanding the belly, instead of the lungs, allows the body to center, ground, relax, and increases the chi, our vital energy.

The hara (dantian or tanden) is the *elixir field*, where energy is created, the center of ki (chi) creative, vital, and sexual energy. It is the sacral chakra, and in Sanskrit, Swadhisthana, located two finger-widths below the navel. As Japanese author and Zen teacher Katsuki Sekida wrote in *Zen Training: Methods and Philosophy*, "It is the correct manipulation of the lower abdomen, as we sit and breathe, that enables us to control the activity of our mind."

In other words, breathing from the Hara can be a gateway to enlightenment, just as sound is a direct pathway to awakening.

Many of my clients in Voice Analysis speak from the upper part of the body, with the sound resonating in the throat and head. This creates a thinner voice tone, without depth, resonance, or power. The deeper harmonics created with Hara breathing and toning are more potent for moving energy, healing, and have a grounding effect. In today's stressful world, buzzing with the multitudes of subtle waves and frequencies of technology, most people need grounding.

When toning, if one imagines the sound and breath arising from the deep cave of the belly, the Hara, the power of this cauldron of fire is projected throughout the body, and the voice expands in depth and with more harmonic overtones. When our voice is fully embodied, with deep, expansive resonance, people listen, and the universe responds to us, hence, manifesting our visions becomes easier. Our voice is constantly informing the world how to respond to us, repatterning our reality. The ancient traditions of sound science have known this for ages, such as the Sufi tradition:

> *"The voice is a barometer of our state of being. The voice indicates one's character and the expression of one's spirit."*
> —HAZRAT INAYAT KHAN, *The Mysticism of Sound and Music*

To practice "Hara Toning", one can use the basic vowels *oh*, *u*, *ah*, *ee*, and visualize the sound rising effortlessly from the Hara up through a hollow bamboo or crystal tube like an internal flute. The tone is not forced but is allowed to emerge effortlessly from the belly, passing through the throat and out the mouth. Try toning from the head and then the belly and compare the tone quality between the two.

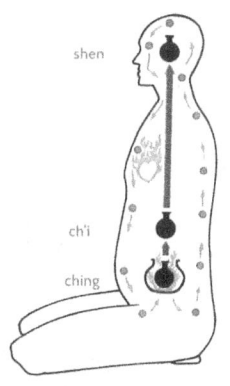

The voice which is grounded in the belly has more potential to resonate the bones, tissues, and stimulate all the energy centers. In Taoism, these subtle centers are called *cauldrons of fire*, as illustrated in the image to the right. The Hara, umbilical center is connected to our origins, the source of nourishment from our mothers and the cord of connection to all of creation. Ancient people believed they could travel to the stars on this umbilical cord, "chord" of connection with all of life.

Another seat of power, the third chakra, *Solar Plexus*, is used in the ancient practice of Nahua Sun Yoga. For many years I worked in Mexico

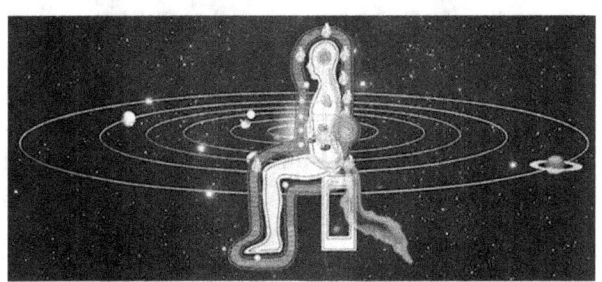

doing concert tours and sound trainings and it was during one of these times that I attended the annual Spring Equinox gathering of Aztec and Mayan elders in Mexico City. The term Nahua basically means *"clear sound or language"* in the Aztec (Nahuatl) language of central Mexico.

To begin, the instructor had us sit in a lotus position, or if needed, in a chair, with back straight, but relaxed, facing the rising sun. He explained the importance of the Solar Plexus, located above the navel and below the diaphragm as a network of radiating nerves, sending information and energy to all parts of the body, like the illuminating rays of the sun. In the Vedic system of India, it is called Manipura, meaning *"lustrous city of jewels, or shining gem."* The instructor guided us to draw the light of the rising sun into the Solar Plexus with our breath for quite some time before circulating the vital force.

This circulating of the vital force is illustrated in the Taoist image on the previous page and is often termed the "micro-cosmic orbit" of Buddhist Tantra practice. Simply following the breath with one's awareness, as it rises and falls, is a simple yet powerful beginning meditation. (Placing the tongue on the roof of the mouth helps to complete the circuit.)

I call this practice the *Golden Cobra* meditation, inspired by the Egyptian initiates who display the cobra uraeus at the third eye. The Egyptian Queen in the image to the right has developed all seven initiatory centers, or chakras, which are illustrated with seven cobras on her crown, and the double Re Herakti of the Rising Sun at her brow.

A variation of Nahua Yoga can be practiced by drawing the rays of the rising sun into the Ajna ("Third Eye") rather than the Solar Plexus, and on the exhale, sending gratitude for the sun's warmth and life-giving radiance. One can imbibe star energy and knowledge from other luminaries, such as Sirius, Antares, or the star of your choice. This is illustrated in the image on the right with starlight entering the Third Eye of the Pharaoh. (Image from the tomb of Tutankhamun.)

© *Ani Williams 2023, Songaia Sound Productions LLC,*
www.aniwilliams.com

Learn more about Voice Spectrum Analysis:

https://aniwilliams.com/voice-spectrum-analysis/

Learn more and listen to Songaia Sound:

https://aniwilliams.com/product/songaia-mp3-set/

APPENDIX VI

The Heart Reconnection Journey: Reclaiming Your Power

A Simple Daily Practice to Transform Your Story

by Sarah Cotterill

PART I: Heart Listening (5-7 minutes)

1. **Connect with your heart center:**
   - Place your hand over your heart
   - Take 3-5 slow, deep breaths
   - Feel your heartbeat against your palm
   - Imagine breathing directly into your heart space

2. **Activate gratitude:**
   - Bring to mind something you're genuinely grateful for
   - Some of my favorites include tulips in the spring, a warm cup of tea, our border collie smiling at me just before a beach run
   - Allow yourself to fully feel this gratitude in your body
   - Notice how this shifts your energy

3. **Heart inquiry:** (Listen for the first answers that arise)
   - "My heart, what do you need from me today?"
   - "My heart, is there an old story within that's ready for a new chapter?"
   - "My heart, what do I need to learn or do to transform this story?"

PART II: Story Transformation (10-15 minutes)

1. **Create a healing narrative:**

   Using the wisdom from your heart inquiry, write a short transformative story using this template or create your own:

   "Once upon a time there was a ___ ___ who ___ ___ .

   They went on an adventure where they learned ___ ___ and returned to their people as a hero who ___ ___ ."

2. **Explore the transformation:**

   How did this experience change your character's relationship with *one* of these aspects of life?

   - Their relationship with work
   - Their approach to health and wellbeing
   - Their connections with others
   - Their creative expression
   - Their sense of purpose
   - Their habit(s) or belief(s)

3. **Embody the wisdom:**
   - What gift is your character now bringing to the world?
   - How can you integrate this wisdom into your life today?
   - What simple action will you take to honor this insight?

Remember

- Stay playful and curious—your brain can't distinguish between imagined and real transformation—so make your story fantastical if you wish
- Trust what emerges—there is no "wrong" story
- Return to this practice regularly whenever you feel stuck, limited, or ready for new possibilities

- This simple practice creates new neural pathways for healing and lasting change with just 15 minutes of regular attention
- Sharing deepens its integration—I'd love to hear your story! Connect with me at:

    https://www.linkedin.com/in/sarah-cotterill-7340a15/

*"The journey of life is moving from
our love of power to the power of love."*

APPENDIX VII

Bilateral Stimulation: A Simple Way to Process Your Emotions

by Mona Sobhani, Ph.D.

Have you ever found yourself instinctively tapping your foot or swaying side to side when feeling anxious? Or maybe taking a long walk helped you clear your mind? These natural movements might be doing more than you realize—they're a form of bilateral stimulation, a technique used to help process emotions and reduce distress.

What is Bilateral Stimulation?

Bilateral stimulation (BLS) refers to rhythmic, back-and-forth stimulation of the brain, using visual, auditory, or kinesthetic (physical) movements. This activates both hemispheres of the brain, helping to integrate and process emotions, memories, and stress. It can be used in everyday situations to promote emotional balance.

Types of Bilateral Stimulation

There are three main types:

1. Visual—Moving your eyes from left to right (e.g., following a therapist's finger or watching a light bar).

2. Auditory—Listening to alternating tones or sounds in each ear (often through headphones).

3. Kinesthetic (Physical)—Engaging in rhythmic movements, like tapping alternate sides of the body, walking, drumming, or even rocking.

How Does It Help?

Bilateral stimulation works by engaging both sides of the brain, which can:

- Reduce emotional intensity of distressing memories
- Help "unstick" the brain when it's overwhelmed by emotions
- Improve problem-solving and emotional clarity
- Promote relaxation and a sense of balance

Everyday Ways to Use Bilateral Stimulation

Even outside of therapy, simple activities can provide the benefits of BLS:

- Going for a walk (the left-right movement of your legs can help process emotions)
- Listening to alternating tones or music in headphones
- Tapping your knees or crossing arms and tapping shoulders in a rhythmic pattern
- Swaying, dancing, or rocking when feeling stressed

Why Does It Work?

The brain processes information more effectively when both hemispheres are activated in a rhythmic way. This is why walking, drumming, or eye movements can make tough emotions feel more manageable. It helps the brain "digest" distressing memories so they no longer feel as overwhelming.

Bilateral stimulation is a powerful tool that leverages rhythm for reducing stress, managing emotions, and even healing trauma. Whether used in therapy or daily life, these simple movements can help bring a sense of calm, clarity, and emotional balance when we need it most.

https://www.monasobhaniphd.com/

APPENDIX VIII

Simple Techniques to Cultivate Love, Forgiveness & Gratitude
by Charles Monroe, Jr.

1. The Rose Technique

I got this from cognitive therapist Bill McKenna. I use this for clients who need to send love and forgiveness to someone. Sometimes the client can't muster up the love to send the person. We use this method instead. I have them imagine a rose in their hand. The rose carries the frequency of love.

In the other hand I have them imagine a living miniature version of the person they need to send love to. Then I have them imagine placing the person gently into the rose and observing the person dissolving into the rose. This method allows them to send the person **to** love as opposed to having to send love to the person.

2. Brain/Heart Coherence Meditation

This one comes from Gregg Braden. It focuses on gratitude and requires the client to place their hands in a prayer mudra over the heart while breathing in slowly for 5 seconds and then breathing out for 5 seconds.

While breathing, I have them imagine all the people in their lives that they are grateful for. I even encourage them to think of those that have passed as well. Imagine them when you saw them at their happiest. It could have been a family event or just laughing at something funny. This signals to the universe that you want more of that feeling and that you want more of that feeling for the person that you are grateful for.

APPENDIX IX

The Triangle: A Conscious Communication Tool
by Deborah Cambio

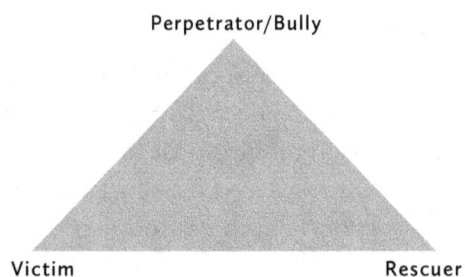

The Triangle is a practical and spiritual communication tool designed by Stephen Krapman, MD* to empower individuals to recognize and transform unproductive roles in their personal interactions. At its core, it identifies three common reactive positions we may take in life situations:

- **The Perpetrator/Bully**—the one who controls, criticizes, or uses force to feel powerful.
- **The Victim**—the one who feels helpless, powerless, wronged; gives away personal responsibility.
- **The Rescuer**—the one who tries to fix or save others.

The Hidden Trap of the Rescuer

The Rescuer often seems kind, caring, or heroic—but this role can subtly take away a sacred opportunity for the other person to learn, grow, or reclaim their own power.

Here's how:

- Rescuing can **disempower others** by implying they are incapable.

- It **interrupts their natural process**, preventing necessary challenges or reflection.

- It **protects us** from feeling uncomfortable with another's struggle or pain.

- It may create **dependency**, reinforcing a cycle of helplessness in the other.

Real Love Allows Space for Someone To Rise

It trusts that the other can find their own wisdom and strength. These roles can arise in our interactions with others—or even within our internal dialogue. Rather than labeling ourselves or others, The Triangle invites compassionate awareness.

What distinguishes this tool is the recognition of two aspects of self:

- **The Actor**—our human, reactive, emotional, ego-based self who plays out roles based on conditioning, wounds, and habits.

- **The Director**—our higher, spiritual self who observes the scene and has the capacity to rewrite the script and redirect the actor.

When we find ourselves caught in any of the Triangle's roles, we pause, acknowledge where we are, and consciously shift our perspective. From the position of the *Director*, we guide the *Actor* to make a new choice—one rooted in awareness, love, and responsibility for a more empowered response.

Importantly, **we can only rewrite our own role**, not the roles others are playing. Our power lies in self-awareness and transformation, not control. By choosing to respond rather than react, we reshape the scene of our life for the highest good.

When we fall into one of the Triangle roles, we:

1. **Recognize** – Become aware of the role we're playing.

2. **Stop** – Pause and create space to reflect.

3. **Redirect** – Our Inner Director will guide the Actor toward a wiser, more empowered response.

Rewriting the Scene

Use these prompts to shift roles:

- Am I trying to fix, control, or blame?
- What is my higher self seeing right now?
- How can I respond with clarity, love, or truth instead?

By stepping out of the reactive role and choosing awareness, we rewrite the story from victimhood or conflict into empowerment and transformation.

The Triangle in Daily Life

Do this when you feel:

- Triggered or upset by someone
- Helping too much
- Stuck in a cycle of blame or self-pity
- Judging yourself harshly

The goal isn't perfection—it's presence.

Each experience in life is a new chance to respond with consciousness.

Closing Thought

"We are not here to control others, but to master our own choices."
When we step into the role of the Director, (Our Higher Consciousness) we reclaim our creative power—and bring more love, truth, and freedom into every experience and scene we live.

* Developed by Stephen Karpman, M.D.

APPENDIX X

What Is Mirroring? How Does It Work? And Why Should You Care?

by Suzy Miller

Mirroring is the phenomenon of something or someone in your environment reflecting back to you something that is held in your unconscious so that it can become conscious.

In the movie *What the Bleep Do We Know*, physicist Fred Alan Wolf, Ph.D., says, "There is no out there out there." Meaning that everything that we experience in our outer landscape is a gift that is attempting to reveal something that we may not be aware of!

Most people do not like the idea of mirroring when it is first presented, because to be aware that our whole lives are reflecting back to us that which has been or needs to be loved and integrated is a wonderful concept only if our lives our beautiful. However, when life is not so easy, the last thing many of us want to do is take ownership of those experiences.

Most of us have been taught from birth that some experiences should be perceived as good and others as bad, and thus, the typical response for most humans when life is not going their way is to point a figure at someone else and say it is their fault. We do this because we feel shame and/or guilt when life is not going as smoothly as we think it should. If we can shift just this one perception we will make a huge difference in our lives and our experience of the world. The reason I believe this is because when you realize that life is bringing up situations that tweak you, not as a punishment, but as an opportunity to love and integrate all aspects of you, it becomes much easier to take those experiences that rub you the wrong way as gifts.

How does mirroring work? Let's start at the level of family. Because of common DNA, behavioral traits, and familial patterns, etc., every member of a family holds different aspects of everyone else. Children are especially good at triggering their parents for this reason. They are not doing it on purpose, but, man, can it feel like they are when their behaviors cause irritation, fear, anger, sadness, or any other negative emotions.

Our human experience is set up for evolution, and the only way we evolve is to become conscious of that which was unconscious. And, thus, the triggering begins. Each time we are triggered by another's behavior, we have inner work to do. There is a wonderful book called *The Presence Process* by Michael Brown, which I highly recommend. In his book, Brown lays out a step-by-step approach to dealing with triggers in such a way that the energy locked inside them can be released, loved, and integrated!

Again, most of us have been conditioned to project our "darker" emotions on to others because it is too scary to own and address them. However, triggers are always an opportunity to feel whatever it is that the trigger brings up. In Brown's book, he offers a four-step process.

1. When triggered, we dismiss the messenger. The person causing the upset is simply doing you a favor by bringing up what has been buried.

2. We give ourselves permission to feel the feeling that arises. Typically, as you feel into the trigger, you will automatically start telling yourself a story, which will provide a clue about what those feelings are connected to.

3. You ask yourself, "When did I last feel this same feeling?"

4. You then ask yourself, "And when, before that, can I recall feeling this feeling?"

Why would anyone want to put this much attention on their emotions? Simple—the more information that you integrate, the more whole you feel. The more whole you feel, the more comfortable energetically sensitive children and adults feel in your presence—and thus, the easier your life with them becomes. For it is not until we heal and integrate our own wounds that we can provide first, the safety, and then the model for energetically sensitive children to be present in this reality.

There are many levels of mirroring, however, I am a firm believer that any individual who does their own emotional body work and becomes more loving toward themselves and others does more for humanity than one hundred people spouting their concepts and ideas for change in others.

APPENDIX X

*Real change happens from the inside out,
one person at a time!*

About the Author

GAIL LYNN is a visionary inventor, author, and trailblazer in frequency healing. She is best known as the creator of the **Harmonic Egg**® and the **LiFT**™ – revolutionary sound and light frequency chambers designed to support mental, emotional, physical, and spiritual well-being through energy resonance and sacred geometry.

Gail's path to innovation began with personal adversity. In 2007, at age 37, she was diagnosed with severe cardiovascular stress—an outcome of years spent navigating high-pressure careers in the automotive, telecommunications, and film industries, as well as challenging personal relationships. This turning point led her to seek alternative methods of healing, sparking her deep dive into energy medicine.

After opening her first light and sound therapy center in Denver, Colorado, in 2010, Gail experienced transformative results through holistic sound and light sessions. As she and her clients began reporting increased intuition, clarity, peace, joy, and a noticeable reduction in anxiety and fear, she knew this was more than a coincidence—it was a blueprint for healing.

ABOUT THE AUTHOR

Determined to merge ancient wisdom with modern science, Gail developed the **Harmonic Egg**®. This immersive healing chamber combines sacred geometry, Tesla mathematics, and consciously composed music by professional musicians. Each element is intentionally designed to harness the body's natural ability to rebalance and restore itself. In 2020, just four years after applying, Gail was awarded a patent for the **Harmonic Egg**. Today, her technologies are used worldwide, inspiring a growing movement of people reclaiming their wellness and reconnecting with the innate intelligence of their bodies.

Gail is also the author of *Unlocking the Ancient Secrets to Healing: Why Science is Looking to the Past for the Future of Medicine*, in which she shares the research and revelations behind her work, and the Executive Producer of the film *It's Time*.

To learn more about Gail Lynn, the **Harmonic Egg**, the film, *It's Time*, and Gail's expanding suite of frequency healing innovations, visit:

https://harmonicegg.com

https://itstime.love

Also by Gail Lynn

"A fascinating account of an extraordinary journey through ancient history, modern science, and the birthing of a revolutionary new sound and light therapy that is helping thousands overcome their health concerns."

AT THE AGE OF 37, Gail Lynn's dream of making a difference in the world was rudely shattered. The accumulated stress of two challenging relationships and three extremely competitive careers in the automotive, telecommunications, and film industries had decimated her physical, emotional, and psychological reserves, leaving her with a medical diagnosis of severe cardiovascular stress.

Determined to restore her health, Gail plunged into the world of energy medicine. When a series of whole-body light and sound treatments reversed her diagnosis, she set out to uncover both the ancient history and modern science behind light and sound as healing therapies.

After opening a light and sound healing center in Colorado in 2010, a series of extraordinary synchronicities guided her to combine light and sound technologies with sacred geometry and Tesla mathematics. The result was a revolutionary vibroacoustic, resonance healing chamber called the **Harmonic Egg**®, which is advancing frequency healing to an unimagined level.

Part memoir, part illuminating treatise on why science is looking to the past for the future of medicine, *Unlocking the Ancient Secrets to Healing* chronicles the personal tribulations and professional discoveries behind the remarkable realization of Gail Lynn's dream.

From her humble beginnings in Detroit, Michigan to a seven-year relationship with Elvis Presley's step-brother, and a role as producer on a Hollywood movie about the "King," to triumphant success stories from world-renowned composers, musicians, professors, and physicians, *Unlocking the Ancient Secrets to Healing* makes riveting and inspiring reading.

Gail Lynn has worked in the automotive, telecommunications, and film industries. She is the creator of the **Harmonic Egg** and the **LiFT**™, these products are giving thousands of people new hope for a quality of life they never imagined.

Gail Lynn also co-created several original music pieces for the **Harmonic Egg**, each piece is limitless in how it can serve the greater good…play with the music, have fun with it, use your intuition, each song includes notes with instructions to get you started on your journey to use music (sound) and colors in your daily life! To learn more, visit:

https://harmonicegg.com

www.ingramcontent.com/pod-product-compliance
Lightning Source LLC
Chambersburg PA
CBHW052139070526
44585CB00017B/1898